ISBN-10: 1915662974
ISBN-13: 978-1-915919-99-1
ASIN: B0BW7QRQJT

© Dr Andrew Rynne 2023

Email: drandrewrynne@gmail.com

Table of Contents

Dedication

This book is dedicated to all the children who suffered
or died at The Caragh Orphanage.

We name them here at the end of the book.

Acknowledgements

We especially want to thank Paul Cooke for his generous contribution in researching this book. Without his help this work may not have been possible.

John Hillis

Irene Houlahan (née Weld.)

Bryan White of Bray

Representative church body library Dublin

Rev. Olive O'Donoghue Athy

National Archives Dublin

British and Irish Newspaper Archive

Séan Curran for the Tandy's Bridge Sketch.

The late Stephen Rynne for Healy's Bridge Sketch

Rev. James Reid

Brid Rynne for Swans Sketch

Ramona Valentine BSc. Hons., IT Support & assistance

Seamus Leahy Kilkenny Courthouse

Introduction

This is the truly bizarre story of a clergyman who exploited the natural trust that people gave and still give to men of his calling. He was able to extract from these trusting people bountiful charitable donations to help *'poor little orphaned children'* held by him in a pseudo-orphanage located beside his Glebe House in Caragh, Co. Kildare. These donations amassed for him and his wife, a fortune at the time.

He established an institution with all the outwards appearances of an orphanage, but that inside revealed a miserable, squalid place not fit for human inhabitation. You will read here how, during court case after court case, reliable witness after witness gave accounts of the most harrowing and unspeakable cruelties being meted out to defenceless children in this filthy place. Cotton and his wife Eliza were well aware of these atrocities but chose to do nothing about them.

In fact, Cotton had what today we call **Antisocial Personality Disorder** or APD. He had all the traits

1

of this mental anomaly, only in his case, they were very severe and unrelenting.

Chief among them were:

· Impulsive irresponsible criminal behaviour.
· Reckless risk-taking.
· Manipulative and deceitful interpersonal reaction.
· Transference of blame that is rightfully theirs onto others.
· No insight into, and denial of, the hurt and pain caused by one's behaviour.
· No remorse.
· An insatiable desire for publicity, however ill-gained.

This might account for Cotton's reoffending so soon after getting out of Mountjoy Jail. He craved the attention that litigation might bring him, irrespective of the consequences.

Antisocial Personality Disorder was not known as this in Cotton's time. This hardly mattered for then, as today, there was no treatment for it other than incarceration. As we will see, this did not work in Cotton's case and rarely does, in fact.

As for the cause of APD, it has been observed that abuse during childhood, either physical or sexual, often leads to this terrible mental deviation. Astute, ongoing, in-depth psychotherapy, along with strong anti-psychotic medication, may help. But the truth is that in Cotton's time, as is the case today, little if anything can be done for APD.

Finally, the question must be asked if there was more that could have been done to save these poor children from such horrible and protracted torture. Certainly, the then recently established Irish Society for the Prevention of Cruelty to Children (ISPCC) played a heroic role in bringing Cotton to book and helping to disperse the children afterwards. Likewise, the local Royal Irish Constabulary (RIC) quickly responded to the ISPCC concerns, investigated them, and followed through with summons and convictions.

What was surprising, however, was the ineptitude of The Church of Ireland's response to Cotton's behaviour. This kind of coverup was (more) typical for most religious institutions then as it still is today. The archbishop was made aware in writing by the church seniors in Kilberry that Cotton was dangerous. This was years before the so-called orphanage was built or a single child was taken into it and damaged!

The Church of Ireland authorities were in a strong position to put some restraints on Cotton's antics. But instead, they chose to do nothing, not even after the 'Reverent Gentleman' was imprisoned for the first time. It was, in fact, not until after the orphanage was evacuated and Cotton was imprisoned for the second time that the church authorities eventually stirred themselves. But it was too late by then. All the damage had already been done.

1 – The Cottons

"The remains of one adult and five children which were removed on 30th October 1976 from Carragh Churchyard are buried here."

In 1976 the remains of several bodies of children were exhumed from around Cotton's church in Caragh and reinterred in a mass grave beside nearby Millicent Church. We do not know the names of these children nor that of the adult buried with them.

****

As you cross the Cock Bridge on the road from Caragh to Blackwood in County Kildare and look over to your right, there behind the ruined house, once a Post Office, are the foundations of the Caragh Orphanage still to be seen today. You could never imagine the unspeakable acts of cruelty which took place here in the latter half of the 19th century and which were the subject of many a sensational court case involving the Reverend Samuel Cotton, once respected Church of Ireland clergyman, and his wife, Eliza. He becomes reviled by both his own flock and the Catholic population of the district. The story of what happened here at the Caragh Orphanage is the subject of this book. At times it makes for difficult reading.

The treatment of illegitimate children and their mothers has been at the forefront of the news in modern times. The recent scandals surrounding the industrial schools, Magdalene laundries, mother and baby homes, and the discovery of hundreds of infants remains in Tuam, County Galway, has shocked and horrified us. But this treatment of the most vulnerable in our society is not the product of recent times. Nor was it the prerogative of Catholic institutions.

****

Samuel George Cotton was born at No 2 St. Georges Place, Bray, in 1823. He was the eldest child and only son of Francis Robert Cotton (1794-1851) of Allenton, Dublin, and Susanna Lucas (d. 1843), eldest daughter of Minchin Lucas of Woodtown, Dublin. His parents were married at Tallaght Church on 1st Jan 1823.

No 2 St. Georges Place, Bray, replacement house to Cotton's birthplace.

Samuel was educated by Mr Flynn in his private school and later went to the School of Divinity in Trinity College, Dublin. He was ordained Deacon for Dublin in Christ Church Cathedral on Sunday, August 22nd, 1847. His first appointment after Ordination was to Athy, County Kildare, as Curate. His ordination (by letters dimissory) to the priesthood took place in the Cathedral Church of St. Mary, Tuam, County Galway, on Sunday, 18th June 1848. He was then appointed to the vicarage of Kilberry, just outside Athy, which had become vacant on the promotion of the previous incumbent, Rev. William Warburton, to the Deanery of Elphin.

He married Eliza Gordon Johnson, youngest daughter of Henry Cavendish Johnson Esq. Major 25th Royal Welsh fusiliers, on December 20th, 1855.

No sooner had Samuel and Eliza married than Samuel started to exhibit what would become a life-long trait. He started bringing people to court for no good reason other than his refusing to have a dialog with the parties involved. He was litigious if given even the smallest excuse. He could hold forth, get attention, and have his name in the papers by going to court.

Church in Kilberry today

Early in their scandalous career, perhaps while in Kilberry, the Cottons probable saw the potential that destitute poor children had for raising charitable donations. Later he assiduously applied this lesson of shamelessly using poor and woefully disadvantaged Catholic babies and children as a magnet for raising soft money while easing people's conscience. Donations to assist helpless, poor children had a strong "feel good" factor associated with it, and so the money poured in.

Here is but one example of Cotton's fundraising exercise making regular appearances in the popular press of the day.

"Saunders's News Letter November 27th, 1868

THANKS. THE CARAGH ORPHANAGE FOR DESTITUTE CHILDREN

Mrs Cotton begs to acknowledge the following:

Friends of A.S. £5. J.P.M. and friends £3,10s Mrs Van Hagan, £3. Rev. D. C. Courtenay (col), £2.12s Lady and George C. Fitzgerald Esq, and Miss Fothergill, £2 each, the Lady Steward Richardson (col) and Mrs Lowry (col), £1 10s, each.

John R Fowler, Esq., J.P., Miss Lambert, Mrs J.P Mrs Hyndman, Mrs Leech, £1 each Mss Green. P.C Cockburn, Esq., Miss L Royston, 10s each, a well-wisher, Mrs Courtenay Newton, Rev. A. Roberta, Mrs Cox, Miss Goodall, Mrs Swan, Mrs Whittaker, Miss Copley, Mrs Turner, Thomas P. Dormer, Esq., 5s each. Miss Wainhouse, 3s, W.W.R. Ferns, Arthur N. Jones, Esq., J.P., Mrs F.F. Carmichael, 2s 6d. each. Mrs Brace, Miss Newport, Mrs King, Miss Nicholson, Rev. J. W. Martin, 2s each. Mr R. Burge and Anon, Banbridge, 1s. each."

Samuel Cotton was an enthusiastic advocate of fundamental Protestantism. He was fanatical and unyielding in his views. He was black and white on all things religious. He entertained no argument or discussion. He was absolutely anti-intellectual. Whenever he perceived any threat to himself, he immediately resorted to the law. He never reasoned or discussed. He preferred litigation and the adversarial system.

He detested Catholicism and considered "saving children from popery" by taking them into his hideous school and orphanage a virtue in itself. For these reasons and many others, he was universally unpopular with his fellow Protestant and Catholic neighbours. He had few, if any, friends. On many occasions, he depended on his in-laws to bail him out of remand prison. Eventually, he had no congregation. And still, he couldn't change nor mend his ways. Almost from the start, the Reverend was not popular with his congregation, and there were clear warning signs that he was trouble.

The following letter, addressed to the Archbishop of Dublin by the parishioners in Kilberry, is an early example of the outrage felt at Cotton's dishonesty, arrogance, and neglect of duty while ministering there. It should have been enough to set off alarm bells but somehow failed to do so.

"TO HIS GRACE, THE ARCHBISHOP OF DUBLIN.

May it please your Grace, we, the undersigned parishioners of Kilberry parish, humbly request that your Grace will be kind enough to cause an inquiry to be made into the conduct of the Rev. S.G. Cotton, vicar of this parish.

His almost total neglect of the parish during weekdays, he more than once neglected to attend the Church on Sunday, and consequently, the parishioners were obliged to return home without church service, his refusal to allow his books to be inspected by his churchwardens, or allowing them to know the disbursements of the charities, his getting a receipt for the payment of a subscription towards the painting of the Church, altered, and keeping a portion of such subscription and more especially, his conduct at a vestry held this day, called by himself, where, with force and violence, he endeavoured to put two of his parishioners out of the porch of the Church, in fact, into his entire conduct as a clergyman.

By your Grace causing this inquiry, you will confer a favour on your Grace's humble servants.

Signed A.G. Judge, George J. Phipps.

Churchwardens, James Butler, J.B. Pilsworth. Thomas Baisely, Mark Cross, R. Warrell, W. Hosking, J. Bailey, Wm. Sherlock, J. Smyth, Benjamin Whittacre."

The letter was verified and supported by a local grandee – Lord Downes, thus:

"The conduct of the Rev. Mr Cotton has for some time past been of such an extraordinary nature, so many circumstances affecting his character have been related to me since my return to the country a fortnight ago, and the fact that many of his parishioners have ceased to attend his church combine to make me hope, that his Grace, the Archbishop, will comply with the request of the parishioners, who have signed this paper and cause an inquiry to be made into the grievances they complain of. Signed Lord Downes Bert House, April 7th, 1855."

What lay behind this letter to his Grace is very telling of Cotton's shocking behaviour in Kilberry from the very start of his ministry if that what you could call it. His immediate predecessor there, was the Rev. William Warburton. William exemplifies all that was best in the ethics of the Church of the day. He was open and honest in collecting charitable funds to relieve famine victims in the area. His books were always open to inspection. Because of this, many people of the district were spared the suffering and indignity of being sent to the workhouse.

William Warburton is eventually moved on, and in his place comes the Rev. Samuel Cotton. Cotton is the very antitheses of his predecessor. He is sneaky and dishonest. He allowed nobody to inspect the books. Not without good reason, some of his parishioners suspect that he is embezzling charitable donations. One can only imagine how galling that would be and the amount of antipathy it would engender.

As always, in a situation where he is cornered, Cotton immediately resorts to the printed media to give his behaviour the varnish of respectability by broadcasting it. In a rambling, self-serving letter to The Leinster Express dated Jan 17th, 1856, he, first of all, blames his boss, The Rev. Trench, Rector of Athy, for not agreeing to mediate in the terrible row started in the first place by Cotton himself. Trench seems to take the view that by his intervening might make matters worse, not better, and that Cotton needs to sort it himself.

Reading through the rest of his diatribe, it becomes abundantly clear that Cotton identifies Messers A.G.

Judge, George Phibbs, and Lord Downes as his nemeses whom he is ready to forgive. And in any case, he is innocent of all charges. He never touched a penny, and his books were open to all and sundry to inspect.

The grovelling letters to his Grace gave a clear signal of things to come. Already his violent and dishonest behaviour was causing great unease among his congregation. It took courage for these men to write in this manner to the Archbishop. One would have expected that on the back of these serious complaints against him, the Archbishop might at the very least have called in Cotton and have given him a much deserved and good dressing down. But there is no record of anything like that ever happening, and Cotton's behaviour continued largely unchecked. Eventually, he is moved on so that another community has to suffer the consequences of his evil ways. That community, the people of The Church of Ireland in Caragh, County Kildare, little know what awaits them. Much worse was to come.

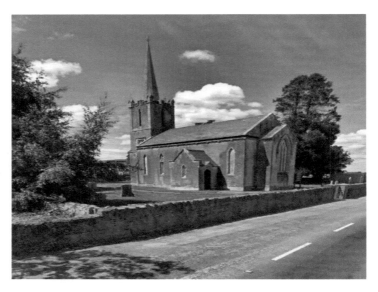

The Church in Kilberry today

The foundation of Caragh Orphanage

What was it that motivated the Cottons to build an orphanage and school designed to cater to the poor and destitute Catholic children of Ireland? The Cottons had no children of their own, and the running of an orphanage was not, it would seem, out of a great need to express love and care for needy children. Neither was it because of their natural aptitude for running institutions like this, as they had absolutely no previous experience in such an enterprise. What inspired them then, to take on the responsibilities and difficulties of running an orphanage?

Evangelisation, saving children from popery, and increasing the Protestant population, may have been part of it. But if it was, it was a very small part. It would seem from the evidence that the Cottons used the orphanage as a conduit to collect money to finance their own comfortable lifestyle, as very little of that which was collected was spent on the care of children. The notion may have had some semblance of credibility had they treated these little children with even a modicum of respect or kindness. But sadly, this was not to be the case.

Baby Farming became common in the 19th century and proved very lucrative for those involved. In the days before the regulation of adoption and fostering, and when illegitimacy was shrouded in secrecies and carried deep social stigmata, it was often viewed as a convenient means of solving a difficult problem for young mothers in distress. Typically, an infant was given up to a wet nurse in exchange for payment, either a lump sum upfront or for ongoing periodic payments, with the expectation that the infant would be cared for by someone other than its own family, and usually for a defined period of time. When this down payment ran out and no more seemed to be forthcoming, babies were left to die in extreme cases.

While many wet nurses genuinely cared for the children placed with them, there are some notorious examples where children were abused and sometimes killed, as the lump sum payment was not enough for the long-term provision of these unfortunate children. The infamous cases of Margaret Waters (executed in 1870) and Amelia Dyer (executed in 1896) illustrate the extremes to which some people would go in order to profit from this 'outsourcing' of infants.

The Cottons would probably today be regarded as baby farmers. The children kept at the Caragh Orphanage were held under an 'Indenture of Apprenticeship', which purportedly bound them to their new masters and removed the mother's right of access to her children, should she change her mind with respect to the 'adoption'.

The Cottons used this Indenture falsely, as apprenticeship did not apply to infants or young children, but usually for trades from the age of 14 to 21, though sometimes children younger than 14 were bound in certain instances. The parents of most of the children taken in by the Cottons were poor and illiterate and thus did not really understand the legality of having their very young children signed over in this manner. In these mothers' eyes, giving up their children was seen as a means of providing for their future in a way that they could not do due to their poverty and circumstance.

In all cases, Cotton was remunerated for the care of each child. This either came from its legal guardian or a sponsoring person. He did not keep any children without payment. Not just that, he also received generous donations from friends and associates who were unaware of what was really going on. Then, as today, the words "little children" were emotional trigger words practically guaranteed to raise charitable donations by appealing to the giver's emotions.

The move to Caragh 1862

Rev. Cotton was transferred from Kilberry to Caragh in March 1862 after a controversial few years in Kilberry marred by deep suspicions and resentment as to Cotton's honesty. A vacancy was presented at Caragh by the appointment of Rev. Arthur Ellis Archer, the previous incumbent, to Donard, County Wicklow. As there was no glebe house in this Union of Caragh, the Cottons resided in Dublin for the first four years until a new glebe house would be erected.

Building a Glebe House 1865-1866

A Caragh Glebe House building fund was begun in 1865 with advertisements placed in major Dublin newspapers requesting donations in order to purchase glebe land and to erect a suitable residence for the Cottons. In reality, the land was gifted, not purchased from Charles A Bury. Within a year, sufficient money had been collected to enable the commencement of work, and the first stone of the new Glebe House was laid on 12th May 1866 by Charles A Bury of Downings House, who was the local landlord and also a churchwarden in Cotton's church. The architect was Joseph Maguire, and the builder was Thomas Holt.[1]

---

[1] Dublin Evening Mail, 16 May 1866

The Archbishop of Dublin having approved of the plans and specification for Caragh Glebe-house, county Kildare, the first stone was laid on the 12th instant|by Charles Bury, Esq., J.P., of Woodville, senior church-warden, in the presence of the architect, Joseph Maguire, Esq., the builder, Mr. Thomas Holt, and some of the parishioners and members of the congregation. When the stone had been pronounced by Mr. Bury to be well and truly laid, the Rev. S. G. Cotton, incumbent, offered up a prayer that the blessing of the Almighty might rest on the future house—that those who were about to engage in the building might be preserved, in the providence of God, from danger or accident, and that it might be a residence for many years to come for a faithful teacher of " the truth as it is in Jesus." The proceedings terminated with the Lord's Prayer and benediction.

Building an orphanage 1866-1867

In August 1864, a position became available with the Dublin Protestant Orphanage Society. The 'Protestant Orphan Society' was founded on 30 November 1828 and was a very carefully regulated Orphan Society that developed a boarding out system and apprenticeship scheme to help the poor Protestant children in Dublin. Rev. Cotton was successfully elected assistant-secretary to this Society. Within twelve months, Rev. Cotton resigned as assistant secretary and, on his resignation, there were one hundred and seven applications for his position.

Barely a week had passed after his resignation from the Dublin Protestant Orphanage Society when the Rev. Cotton was placing advertisements in national and international papers calling for moral, upright members of the public to prevail in donating to his cause in helping with god's work as he set the structures in place for building an orphanage at Goatstown, Caragh in County Kildare which would become known as the Caragh Orphanage.

The Reverend Cotton, it seems, had perfected his ability to raise bountiful donations, a skill perhaps he worked on while employed as assistant secretary in Dublin. The Dublin Protestant Orphanage Society had a well-oiled system of governance with clear guidelines and structures. The orphanage near Caragh was far from that. Although the children were instructed in the Protestant faith, it was not part of the Church of Ireland. It was a private entity run by the Cottons and provided for by generous if somewhat misguided subscriptions.

Even during these very early days of his ministry in Caragh, it seems that he was not popular with his congregation. So unpopular indeed was Cotton that these good people decided not to attend the Church in Caragh but to move their place of worship into Downings House. The drawing room there was consecrated by the bishop for that purpose.

Here we have the Vestry Notes made in Cotton's own writing and taken over a period of four years giving witness to the fact that the Church in Caragh was void of any parishioners:

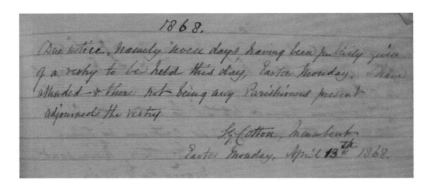

We can only speculate as to why Cotton's congregation abandoned him en masse. However, it is very tempting to believe that they had had word up from Kilberry about his behaviour while there. Ireland is but a village, and news spread quickly then as now.

Downings House to where worship was moved shortly after Cotton's arrival in Caragh

Charles A Bury, Local Magistrate, Downings House

2 - Pistol shooting at the boy. Hooligans at the door. Fighting with canal workers. Overcharging Taxi.

Robertstown County Kildare

Here we give you a few short anecdotes, taken from the press of the day, giving some insights into Cotton's aggressive and reckless manner in response to very little provocation.

At the Robertstown petty sessions, before Sir Gerald G. Aylmer. Bart., S.G Ireland and Charles Wright. Esq. (later Bury) March 20th, 1869.

John McEvoy of Newtown Donore, County Kildare was passing along the road with Edward Donnelly. He met Mr Cotton and cried out, "ha, ha, Cotton". He said that Mr Cotton drew a pistol out of his pocket. McEvoy ran into the shrubbery, and when he was in the shrubbery, he stated that he heard a shot. His back was then to Mr Cotton, and when he turned around, Mr Cotton had a pistol in his hand. It was pointed downwards, according to John McEvoy.

McEvoy said that there were two ladies with Mr Cotton, and when he got the chance, he then ran away. McEvoy said there were about fifteen or sixteen boys around at the time, but he was the only one that insulted Mr Cotton, affirming that it was the first time he had ever insulted him. Edward Donnelly corroborated McEvoy's evidence.

Mr Montgomery submitted there was no evidence to go to the jury against Mr Cotton. It was not proved by any of the witnesses that he had pointed the pistol at McEvoy.

However, the Judge held there was evidence, and a case was set forth.

Mr Montgomery addressed the jury for Mr Cotton, after which Miss Margaret Johnson (Eliza Cotton's sister) was examined by Mr Walker. She stated she was in company with Mr and Mrs Cotton on the day, and a number of people were shouting at Mr Cotton in an insulting manner. McEvoy ran away. Donnelly gave his name to Mr Cotton but refused to give McEvoy's name.

Miss Johnson said that she frequently heard people shouting when passing the Glebe House gate and that Mr Cotton had a pistol and fired it, but he did not say blood would be spilled or that he would shoot anyone.

Robert Smith deposed that on the evening in question, he met McEvoy dancing up the road calling most insulting names to the Rev. Mr Cotton who was following him with a pistol. He saw McEvoy was running away from Mr Cotton. He went on through the shrubbery and out through the other side. When Mr Cotton got into the shrubbery, he could not see McEvoy, who at this stage had gone into a stubble ditch and hid there. While in the ditch and facing backwards, a shot was fired, apparently from the Newtown Donore direction.

Mr Montgomery summed up on behalf of Mr Cotton and Mr Battersby on behalf of the Crown. The Judge then charged the jury, who acquitted the Rev. Cotton.

This tells us something about Cotton's usual behaviour. For a clergyman of his time, to carry a pistol around in his pocket and use it must have been unusual. It demonstrates immaturity, paranoia, and quickness to violence.

****

It was midnight on Sunday, March 28th, 1869, when the orphanage was attacked by a group of hooligans. What motivated this is anyone's guess. There was an attempt to force in the doors and windows. The "old woman in charge," was Anne Higgins, aged 72. She was the widow of Sergeant Higgins. It was reported that he was honourable discharge from the British army. Rev. Cotton had given her shelter in the Caragh School, believing it inappropriate that she should end her days in the Poorhouse. The attack went on for the best part of an hour, but their efforts to break in were unsuccessful. Eventually, they gave up. What was behind this attack isn't clear. The papers of the day dismissed the attackers as mere hooliganism.

Next, we have an incident on the canal bank near the orphanage.

One afternoon Mr Cotton was riding along the canal bank. According to his own evidence in court, he was visiting parts of his parish delivering tracts. He came upon two men repairing the canal where the side had broken down. Their horses were tethered and blocking Cotton from passing.

A normal person in a situation like this might have said something like:

"Excuse me, gentlemen, your horses are blocking my way. Would you mind moving them, please?"

But Reverend Cotton was not a normal person. Instead, an altercation immediately ensued, with Cotton trying to barge his way through, not waiting for the men to move their horses.

This naturally drew the ire of the workmen who tried to restrain Cotton by grabbing his horse's reins while Cotton defended himself with his horsewhip and lashed out at the men. They threatened to throw Cotton into the canal. The whole unseemly and unnecessary fracas ended in Court in Robertstown, where the case was dismissed.

Finally, we have the taxi overcharging. I'll let the paper of the day tell the story:

"REV. MR. COTTON AND THE CARMAN. – At the Naas Town Court on Monday morning, before Dr. R. S. Hayes, J.P., the Rev. Mr Cotton, of Carogh Orphanage and Glebe, prosecuted a carman named Edward Moran, residing in Naas, for a breach of the town commissioners' by-laws, inasmuch as the defendant demanded more than his legal fare.

There was also a second charge preferred against the carman of using obscene and abusive language to the complainant. It appeared that the Rev. Mr Cotton's servant girl hired the defendant at Sallins Railway Station to proceed to Carogh, the agreement being that he was to receive the sum of 5s. for the journey. On reaching the destination, however, the complainant offered the defendant 3s., which he said was the legal fare for the distance. The defendant refused to accept the amount tendered and became most violent, using very strong language, in fact, the 'contretemps' was very near ending in blows. The complainant said he endeavoured to pitch the carman out of the hall-door,but stated that he did not know he had such a Hercules to deal with. The defendant was fined in the sum of £1 – being 10s. for each offence, or the alternative of one month."

REV. MR. COTTON AND THE CABMAN.—At the Naas Town Court on Monday morning, before Dr. R. S. Hayes, J.P., the Rev. Mr Cotton, of Carogh Orphanage and Glebe, prosecuted a carman named Edward Moran, residing in Naas, for a breach of the town commissioners' by-laws, inasmuch as the defendant demanded more than his legal fare. There was also a second charge preferred against the carman of using obscene and abusive language to the complainant. It appeared that the Rev. Mr Cotton's servant girl hired the defendant at Sallins Railway Station to proceed to Carogh, the agreement being that he was to receive the sum of 5s. for the journey. On reaching the destination, however, the complainant offered the defendant 3s., which he said was the legal fare for the distance. The defendant refused to accept the amount tendered, and became most violent, using very strong language, in fact, the *contretemps* was very near ending in blows. The complainant said he endeavoured to pitch the carman out of the hall-door, but stated that he did not know he had such a Hercules to deal with. The defendant was fined in the sum of £1—being 10s. for each offence, or the alternative of one month.

3 – The escape of Elizabeth Daly

Main Street Naas

The next time we find Mr Cotton annoying the local constabulary is in the Elizabeth Daly case. This little girl, Elizabeth Daly, about ten years of age, escaped the Caragh Orphanage in October 1871 and walked all the way to Naas via the canal bank, a distance of some six miles. She got herself as far as the Harbour in Naas, where she sought employment as a servant girl from a Mrs Manders.

One might expect that the Reverend Cotton or his wife Eliza would be sick with worry and concerned for the child's welfare. As it turns out, the Cotton's only concern seems to be the fact that Elizabeth had "stolen a quantity of wearing apparel, his property".

They were the only clothes she had, and now he wanted this child arraigned before the magistrates charged with stealing his property. 'Wearing apparel' is a very fancy name for the rags usually given to these children. These actions may give us an idea of how the Cotton's twisted, perverted logic worked. It is also a window into the realities of what the Caragh Orphanage was really all about.

A child absconds and goes missing. And is he worried about her welfare or even her whereabouts? Not at all. His greatest concerns are for the rags she is wearing and his property. Mr Cotton now asks for the bench to have the case remanded to Kilmeague petty sessions. Mr French stated he had no objection to complying with Mr Cotton's request, and the case was accordingly remanded to Kilmeague petty sessions.

Constable Kelly stated that the warrant is at present in the hands of the constabulary of that district.

Alleged Larceny

The Rev. S. G. Cotton, Incumbent of Caragh, applied to the bench for an order to have Elizabeth Daly remanded to Kilmeague petty sessions on the charge of having absconded from the Caragh Orphanage and stolen a quantity of wearing apparel, his property.

Mr Cotton, on entering the witness box, refused to be sworn on the Testament used in the court because it had a cross on the cover. He refused to be sworn on it and produced his own Testament book and was accordingly sworn thereon. The cross in question was roughly in the shape of a Celtic Cross, which he found objectionable.

He deposed that the accused Elizabeth Daly, aged about ten years of age, disappeared from the Caragh Orphanage school on the morning of Tuesday, October 16th and have done every possible search, he was unable to discover where she went. He offered a reward of £2 for her recovery.

Subsequently, on seeing the advertisement for the reward, Constable McKenna made inquiries around the town and found that the girl had called to Mr Carroll's house near the harbour in Naas looking for employment. Constable McKenna went to Mr Carroll's house, and he, Carroll, explained to the Constable that he had no situation to offer the child but did, however, direct her to the house of Mrs Manders in Naas. This is where Constable McKenna found the young girl and brought her back to Mr Cotton's orphanage.

4 - Kate Kelly Keogh: Infanticide

Kate Kelly is walking from the Cock Bridge down towards Digby Bridge and on towards the aqueduct where the Grand Canal crosses the River Liffey. She is headed back for Naas in County Kildare. It has been raining all this day, Friday, January 19th, 1883. Some gorse bushes to her right are venturing out into early bright yellow flowers. Dabchicks swimming on the canal appear and disappear as she approaches. Under her black woollen shawl, borrowed that morning from her friend Mrs Hanlon, Kate Kelly carries her two babies, one in each arm held warm and close to her breast as she speeds along. These twin girls, Mary, and Brigid Kelly, were born to Kate some nine days previously in the workhouse in Naas. They are strong, healthy babies, and the burden of carrying them grows with each passing step.

When she reaches the aqueduct, now over halfway into her journey, she sits on the low wall there. She must rest. The rain has stopped at last. Her shoulders move up and down as she sobs convulsively and inconsolably, for she is alone in the world. Kate Kelly is deeply distressed. Her husband died three months ago, and now, along with her three other children, she has these little twin babies to cope with. She is at a breaking point.

Someone had told her that the Reverend Samuel Cotton kept an orphanage in Caragh some six miles west of Naas. This may be her last hope. She can't cope with five children, all under the age of six, and she is without any support or means. She is near destitute. Starvation faces them all unless she can get some help now. When she arrived at the Caragh Orphanage, the reception was cold and indifferent. She was told that the Reverend Samuel could no longer take in babies since they were a drain on scarce resources. If she was prepared to pay two pounds, then he might consider taking the babies in. But beyond that, Cotton had nothing to offer.

Kate then pleaded with Eliza Cotton, hoping that she, as a woman, might be more sympathetic to this little family's plight. In this, however sadly, she was much mistaken. Eliza agreed with her husband. There was no longer any place in their orphanage for babies, and they must return from wherever they had come from.

Now she is on her way again and resumes her terrible journey. She passes Soldier's Island on her left at the junction between the main canal and the Naas Branch canal. Dark thoughts are filling her head. She wants to drive them out but can't. She loves her twin babies with all the love that only a mother is capable of. She must not harm these beautiful little girls.

Now she crosses the branch canal by taking a sharp left turn over Tandy's Bridge and then an immediate right heading for Naas Harbour by the canal bank. The canal is now to her right, and the Naas Gasworks some fifty yards ahead of her on the left. Here she pauses and lays her babies gently on the ground on the canal's edge.

Picking up her baby daughter Mary, Kate loosens the child's warm woollen cardigan and finds nearby a stone of about four pounds in weight. This she secures under the baby's cardigan and fastens into position. Now she lowers her daughter into the canal. The water here is about two feet deep. Weighed down by the stone, Mary is doomed. She cannot swim nor escape. She flays her little arms and legs about in a futile effort to save herself. Soon tiny bubbles escape her mouth and nose and rise to the canal's surface. Then all is quiet. The baby is still, blue, dead.

Now the mother gathers her second child Brigid into her arms. This time she is too distressed to look for a stone but lowers her baby into the canal waters without further ado. Again, as her sister had done, baby Brigid flays her tiny limbs about. But it is hopeless. Tiny bubbles soon escape her mouth and nose, there is an eerie silence, and she too, like her tiny sister, is dead.

Kate Kelly Keogh is later arrested and brought up to the Petty Sessions.

Kate Kelly/Keogh is charged with Child Murder

On February 28th, 1883, Constable Cummins discovered in the canal the body of a female child. The body was in an advanced state of decomposition, and a stone weighing 4lbs 11oz was secured inside her clothing. The canal lies between Mr Cotton's residence and Naas.

Kate Kelly, alias Keogh was indicted for the wilful murder of her infant child, Mary Kelly alias Keogh, on January 19th last. She pleaded not guilty, and Mr David Sherlock (instructed by Mr Brown) was assigned by the Crown to defend her. The evidence against the prisoner was a repetition of that given at the Petty Sessions on Monday. Mr Sherlock addressed the jury for the defence. He contended against conviction in that the prisoner must either have thrown the children into the canal in a fit of puerperal fever or that their death was caused by negligence.

Tandy's Bridge. By kind permission of Sean Curran Naas.

Kate is sentenced to be hanged

Chief Justice Morris, addressing the grand jury, said that bills of indictment in eight cases would be submitted to them, all of them unimportant characters, except one very sad case, in which an unfortunate woman stands charged with the murder of her infant child, by drowning it in the canal. From the evidence, it appeared that in the month of December last, the prisoner gave birth to two female children in Naas Workhouse. After quitting the workhouse, she went to lodge with a Mrs Hanlon in the town of Naas. On the morning of January 19th 1883, she left Mrs Hanlon's house taking her two infant children with her to leave them, as she said, with the Reverend Mr Cotton, of Caragh, to be taken into his orphanage or school.

That evening she returned without the children. And stated that she had left them with Mr Cotton for four years and that she had "hard work to get him to take them".

It transpired afterwards that Mr Cotton had not taken the children, although it appeared that the prisoner had gone to his residence and had made an application to have them taken under his care.

Here we have Cotton rushing into public print as is his wont. Now, as ever, he is exonerating himself and blaming others for this tragedy that has just come to light. Twin babies have been murdered that he had just rejected, yet he is complaining about nobody supporting him, and if he had received more money, this would not have happened.

"TO THE EDITOR OF THE DAILY EXPRESS.

Sir, I ask permission to add to your report of the trial of the woman Keogh now under sentence of death for child murder. It was utterly impossible for us here to admit the infants into the orphanage. We have no arrangements or staff for nursing, and we close our accounts for 1882 with more than £70 out of pocket, being responsible for 31 children.

The infant's left on the premises from time to time we have been obliged to give out to be nursed. We have frequent applications from mothers anxious to leave us their babies, and if the Christian public aids us, we will open a crèche (or cradle) and save inhuman mothers from the crime of murder or desertion. A similar institution has been working for some time in London with marked success, rescuing the innocent offspring of guilty parents, and enabling unfortunate mothers to recover their characters and earn their bread respectable.

*I am, sir, your obedient servant. S.G Cotton
Rector and vicar."*[2]

On handing down the death sentence to Kate, the
judge said:

*"Kate Kelly alias Kate Keogh, you have been
convicted by the jury of the crime of murder;
and I now become the mere minister of the law
in pronouncing the sentence of death upon you.
I shall not proceed to aggravate the position
you are unfortunately placed in by making any
comments. The evidence submitted to the jury
compels them, I have no doubt most
unwillingly, to find you guilty of murder, but
that conclusion was irresistible, and they could
arrive at no other.*

*The jury has recommended you to mercy, and
that recommendation I shall forward to the
representative of the Queen, with whom it lies
as to whether the recommendation shall be*

---

[2] Kildare Observer and Eastern Counties Advertiser Caragh Glebe
House, March 19th, 1883

complied with or not. It remains for me to pass upon you the sentence which the law requires."

The Judge then put on the black cap.

"The sentence of the law is that I so hereby adjudge and award to you, Kate Kelly, alias Kate Keogh is taken from the bar at which you now stand to the place from whence you came, the prison of Naas and that you be taken on Friday, April 20th 1883 to the place of execution within the walls of the prison in which you are then confined, and that you then and there be hanged by the neck till you are dead, and that your body shall be buried within the walls of the prison within which you shall last be confined after your conviction.

May God have mercy on your Soul."

Kate Kelly escaped a death sentence, and in March 1888, she was released from Prison after serving five years. Days after her release, she left Ireland and emigrated to Philadelphia via Liverpool. She lives the rest of her life in America.

5 - The Logging Case

THE REVD MR COTTON

The Cottons and a selection of orphans awaiting trial in Robertstown.

Sometime around August 1st, 1883, four children escaped the Caragh Orphanage led by Ellen Kelly, aged 12 going on 13. With her were William Nolan and boys John Ross and John Cleary. They were hungry, barefooted, dressed in rags, dishevelled, unkempt and malnourished. Outside of the orphanage, they were obvious and stood out a mile as escapees from the Caragh Orphanage. To avoid detection, therefore, they took the towpath along the Grand Canal, heading due west. When they reached the first bridge, Healy's

Bridge or, more properly, Bonynge Bridge, they took to the road the short distance to Scully's field.

In Scully's field, they dug up some potatoes by hand before returning with them to the canal bank and proceeding westwards. This will show you just how starving these poor children were that they contemplated eating raw potatoes to relieve their hunger.

Onwards they went through Robertstown and Lowtown until they eventually reached the RIC Barrack on the canal bank at Killina just outside the village of Allenwood. Now they were about six miles from the orphanage and gone for over six hours. Here they were picked up by police and returned to the orphanage, their brief escapade is over. Logging was to be their punishment. Logging was then the illegal act of spanceling children with a chain padlocked to their ankle and a heavy log tied to the other end.

Healy's bridge by Stephen Rynne 1942. Healy's house to the left a onetime shebeen.

Head Constable O'Sullivan bends his head into the biting easterly wind. He is walking the towpath along the Grand Canal from Robertstown eastwards towards the Caragh Orphanage. He is in the middle of County Kildare. Some gorse bushes are still in bloom to his left, and a brace of swans glide along the canal to his right. He is making his way from the RIC barracks in Robertstown to the Cock Bridge, near Prosperous in County Kildare. It is Wednesday, August 2nd, 1883, and Constable O'Sullivan is on a mission.

He is about to pay an unannounced visit to the nearby Caragh Orphanage. The recently established Irish Society for the Prevention of Cruelty to Children (ISPCC) had been receiving complaints of a serious nature that some children in the orphanage were being abused. The Society asked that the local constabulary investigate this on their behalf. This is probably one of the first ever investigations carried out at the request of Society.

A brace of swans on the canal by Brid Rynne.

O'Sullivan would have had no idea of what awaited him as he entered the grounds of the orphanage. Looking over to his left, he saw a boy of about eight or nine years of age who was out in a field. He seemed to be dragging something along the ground with his leg. On closer inspection, it turned out that the young boy's ankle had been chained to a substantial log and secured around his ankle by a padlock. He was barefooted and barelegged. The boy's name was William Nolan. The chain seemed to eat into his flesh. O'Sullivan later found out that the Reverend Cotton held the key to this padlock.

The constable, on locating the Reverend gentleman, approached him and asked him if he might explain to him how come he could spancel children like this against the specific provisions of the Infant Life Protection Act 1872. Did he not know that such an act of cruelty to children was now unlawful and subject to prosecution and fine, if convicted?

Reverend Cotton's response to this was one of total nonchalance. His attitude seemed to be that William Nolan had escaped from the orphanage two days earlier along with three other children. How then were these children to be punished and prevented from escaping again? Did Constable O'Sullivan have a better idea? Cotton was, as ever, in denial and up on his high horse.

So, in Cotton's mind, criminal acts of cruelty towards defenceless children were alright so long as the means justified the end. He had at this stage been in the business of caring for destitute orphans for eighteen years, so it is just not credible that he would have been unfamiliar with laws protecting children. The Act had been in effect at this stage for some eleven years. And yet, in talking to the constable, he displayed neither remorse nor any sense of guilt.

In fact, he asked the constable if he had a better idea. It did not seem to occur to him that rather than punishing and chaining up little children, treating them with some respect and occasional kindness may have been a better approach. Because had these children been properly clothed, properly fed and been given even basic creature comforts like some fires and comfortable beds to sleep in at night, then it is doubtful if they would have attempted to escape in the first place. There would have been little motivation for them to take such a risky course of action with such an uncertain outcome.

Thirteen days later, on August 15th Constable O'Sullivan made a second visit to the Caragh Orphanage, this time accompanied by a colleague Constable Bethel. On this occasion, they discovered two boys named John Ross and John Cleary, aged about eight years, chained together by the ankles, with one of them further chained to a log. Both boys were barefooted and barelegged. They were down on their knees, weeding the gravel in front of the Glebe House.

When questioned about this, Cotton again adapted his 'couldn't care less' attitude and wondered what all the fuss was about. After all, these two boys, along with two other children, had some days previously run away and escaped the orphanage. How was he supposed to stop this from happening again?

It says a lot about the Rev. Cotton's character that he had almost two weeks to think about this. He had already been warned by Constable O'Sullivan that what he was doing was illegal and punishable if convicted. A more rational mind might have discontinued hobbling children and have learned his lesson. But that was not Cotton. He never learned anything from experience. He never changed. He never admitted to being wrong.

Now outside, the Constables were approached by a girl named Ellen Kelly, aged 12 years. She said to them, "I had that log on me night and day, from August 2nd to August 11th, and I had to assist in the work of the house during all of that time". This was given in evidence by O'Sullivan during the subsequent trial.

The Constable asked that the log be given to him, which the Rev. Cotton refused to do. He claimed that it was his private property. He did, however, allow it to be weighed. A scale was produced, and the log and chain and padlock weighed 4lbs and 12ozs. Later this log would be produced in court and be described by the solicitor for the prosecution as 'an instrument of torture'.

On Tuesday, August 28th, Reverend Samuel Cotton was first arraigned before the Petty Session of the Magistrates Court in Kilmeague. He was charged with '*committing an aggravated assault on four orphan children*'. This was stern, almost emotive, language. It seemed to indicate the serious, no-nonsense view that the magistrates were taking of Cotton's behaviour.

As it turned out, the case could not proceed on this day. Rev. Cotton found the reason for objection on the following grounds:

- He could not be defended as his solicitor Mr Toomey was on holidays.
- He had not been given sufficient time to read the charges against him.
- He objected to the presence of one of the magistrates on the bench. According to Cotton, Mr Charles Bury of Downings House, a near neighbour of his, bore a grudge against him. They had had a falling out over the sale of potatoes to the orphanage, and legal action was being considered.

A good deal of interest was manifested in the proceedings, as it was known the Reverend Samuel George Cotton, a Protestant clergyman and president of the Caragh Orphanage, was to appear in several summon cases.

The Reverend Samuel George Cotton, who is a gentleman of about 55 years of age, was summoned at the suit of the police.

The Head Constable of the village being the chief prosecutor, for having, on August 15th, committed, in the words of the summons, "an aggravated" assault upon an orphan boy named William Nolan and others.

There were similar summonses mentioning four or five other names against the Rev. gentleman.

When the cases were about to be called, the Rev. Cotton, addressing the bench, said he had been summoned by the police, and he was entitled to have a copy of the information upon which summonses were issued. He had written for a copy of the information but did not get them.

Captain Waring said he could get the information to read over.

Mr Rice, the Petty Sessions Clerk, then handed the defendant a complimentary copy of the evidence.

While the defendant was engaged in reading over the evidence, which was not read out in court and was not allowed to be inspected by the reporters, the Magistrates disposed of the ordinary petty session's cases.

Several little boys and a few girls, stated to be the orphans, were in court and sat on seats some few feet away from the defendant. They all appeared to be in good health and spirits.

THE REV. SAMUEL G. COTTON.

The Defendant, addressing the magistrate, said he laboured under a great disadvantage. He had only received a copy of the evidence, which contained a great deal of matter, that day. He had no means of studying this information and had a solicitor whom he intended to have present Mr Toomey, but he was away on vacation. There is a very fair bench before him now, he stated, but he must ask Mr Bury to retire. It is not necessary for him to give the reasons why he asked this, but he thought he would not act justly toward him.

Mr Curling, the county inspector, said he had no objection to a postponement. The defendant said there were some litigations between Mr Bury and himself; however, Mr Bury said that was not so that there was no litigation between them, and he declined to retire from the bench. The supposed litigation was in respect of the sale of potatoes to Mr Cotton by Charles Bury.

Bury didn't move but held firm. However, his other objections had to be considered reasonable, and Cotton's wish was granted, and the case adjourned for two weeks.

On Tuesday, September 11th, 1883, the case against Cotton was resumed before the Petty Session of the Magistrates Court in Kilmeague. This time Reverend Cotton had his defence solicitor Mr Toomey in court, he had had time to read through the charges, and at his request, the Magistrate he found objectionable, Charles Bury had come off the bench though he remained in court.

The school in Kilmeague, still there, also doubled as a courthouse.

It now became clear to Cotton and to his solicitor that however cavalier an attitude Cotton may have had towards his own behaviour in chaining logs to children's ankles and chaining them together, this was not shared by the bench. The likelihood is that Mr Toomey had severe words with Cotton before this hearing commenced advising him to tone down his arrogant way a bit. Because some of the exchanges between the solicitor for the prosecution Mr Lord and for the defence, Mr Toomey, clearly indicate that the defence was on the back foot.

Toomey tried to contend that the children's behaviour was so bad as to justify their punishment.

Mr Toomey tried to argue that the children had run away, taking with them clothes belonging to Mr Cotton, suggesting that the children were stealing. Mr Lord asked if the children were supposed to go naked like Zulus. Toomey had no answer to this witty comment so instead changed tack.

Mr Toomey asked if the bench thought that the system of punishment by way of logging was not a proper one, then Mr Cotton was perfectly willing to give an undertaking that he would never use it again. As to it being an aggregated assault, the idea was preposterous.

This exchange would seem to indicate that Toomey was saying things that his client would never have agreed to. Cotton was not a man to ever give undertakings to modify his behaviour simply because there was nothing wrong with his behaviours in the first place, at least as far as he was concerned.

Another approach Toomey took in his efforts to defend Cotton was to compare logging with flogging. He contended that logging was kinder than flogging since the former could be measured and quantified while the latter clearly could not.

However, what merits or otherwise of this argument may have had, and it had some, the problem was that in 1883 flogging was legal while logging was not.

At this stage in the proceedings, the prosecution produced the log, chain and padlock as worn by Ellen Kelly for nine days. Mr Ford placed it on a table before the bench. It clattered as it settled down. This produced a loud gasp of horror from the packed courtroom. People at the back had to stand up to get a proper look. The drama was building up. The actual horror of what Cotton had done was sinking in.

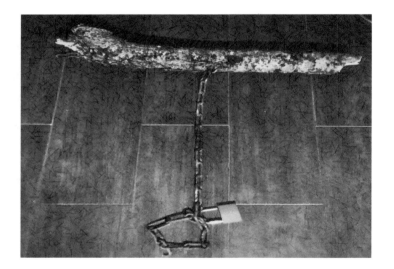

Addressing the bench Mr Lord said:

"We have seen the originals now, and I do hope we will never see them again. I presume your worships have looked at them minutely. I say it is monstrous that anything of the kind should be allowed. Imagine what would be the feeling of any father or mother if they thought for a moment that these blocks were attached to their child's leg, at night as well as day!"

Mr Toomey interposed, "Pardon me, but I object to this sort of statement".

Mr Lord replied, "I have a perfect right to make a statement, and I will promise to this court that I am not stating anything that I cannot prove. I will prove my statement by facts, and I respectfully ask your worships to put a stop to this reprehensible practice and return the reverend defendant for trial to another tribunal, or else dispose of the case summarily under the section of the act of parliament that I have pointed out to you. If this is not done, all I can say is, God protect the poor helpless orphans. But I have every confidence that this court, by their decision here today, will show that they are anxious to put a stop to this shocking crime and that they will not allow it to be tolerated. Now I propose to go into evidence."

"Behold this instrument of torture. Can you just imagine the feelings of the poor little girl who had to drag this after her, night and day, for nine days?" Head constable O'Sullivan, stationed at Robertstown, was examined. He was deposed to going on two occasions to the Caragh Orphanage and finding some of the children logged. The chains were fastened and locked together around the bare leg.

Mr Cotton, whose attention had been called to the matter, refused to give up the blocks, as he said they were his private property. He had to get a facsimile made of one of the blocks, which weighed 4lbs, 12 oz.

One girl named Ellen Kelly had a block on her legs for nine days and nine nights. He (constable) examined her leg and found a scratch on it. On cross-examination, O' Sullivan said Mr Cotton had given him every facility to investigate the case. He had a medical gentleman there to examine the children on the last occasion when he went to the institution. However, he was refused admission as Mr Cotton said it would cause insubordination amongst the children.

Mr Cotton came to the police barracks regarding some of the boys who had run away. He had them charged with larceny. The boys were arrested by the police at Allenwood and brought back, the charges of larceny not having been preferred against them.

Constable O'Sullivan informed Mr Cotton that it was not right for him to be giving so much trouble to the police. He thought Mr Cotton was trying to make fools of the police. One day he came and asked for the whole available men in the barracks.

Ellen Kelly, the little girl who was logged, deposed that she lived at the Orphanage and was about thirteen years of age.

In the month of August last, a chain with a log of wood attached was put around her bare leg by Mr Cotton. It remained on her for nine days and nine nights. She had it on her in bed and doing other domestic work. Her leg was only hurt a little by the chain. Mr Cotton had the key to the lock on the chain, and on one occasion, he was away for two days and said she never made any complaint to Mr Cotton that the chain hurt her leg. She said she rolled in a barrel to move around sometimes, and it was by rolling that her leg was scratched. "The log was put on to keep me from running away. I made the two boys, John Cleary, and

John Ross, go and steal potatoes. That was on the day the log was put upon me."

Mr Toomey asked what did you do with the block when he went out? In answering, the young girl said, I lift it with my hand, and I did the same thing when I had to go upstairs. Turning to the bench, she said, I still live with Mr Cotton.

Mr Nicholson asked her if this was the only thing Mr Cotton ever did to her. Here she told of the floggings she often gets and how Mr Cotton flogged her for making the boys steal the potatoes. She said she couldn't get away from him when he was flogging her because the log was upon her, but he did not take her clothes off her when he was flogging her.

The two boys were then called to the bench. Mr Toomey said he was unaware that the boys would be examined in the case. However, he had no objection to that. On the contrary, he would show that Mr Cotton was willing to give every facility to investigate the case.

William Nolan deposed that he lived in the Caragh Orphanage. He remembered having been logged in the month of August last and that the chain was secured by lock and key. He explained that he was now two years in the orphanage and that he originally lived in Dublin. He said he was a printer now and able to compose type. He learned how to print and type while in the Caragh Orphanage. He said he was learning the trade at the Orphanage and produced a copy of the "Protestant Record" to show how he printed some of it.

He then answered questions asked of him about his age. He said, "I was about fourteen years of age. I ran away to Allenwood on one occasion, but the police brought me back". When they found him on the canal bank at Killina, Mr Cotton tied a log to his leg to prevent him from running away again because he would not make a promise that he would not run away again. When he was running away, he stopped to get some sweets at Robertstown in Mr Cotton's name but was deposed that he was not told to get them. Mr Lord asked what reason you had for running away. (The young boy commenced to cry.) I suppose you were too happy in the orphanage. Mr Toomey interjected, saying there is no use in these insinuations at all.

The hearing was drawing to a close. A final witness, Margaret Conlon, had taught in the orphanage for 12 years. Her evidence was largely self-serving and defensive. She had nothing good to say about Ellen Kelly and seemed to be an apologist for the Cottons. On balance, her evidence contributed little to the defence or to the prosecution. The magistrates now retired to consider their verdict.

Cotton was found guilty as charged and fined £2 each for his attack on the three boys and £4 for logging Ellen Kelly.

In today's values, £10 in 1883 would be well in excess of £1,000, and in 1883 the buying power of £1,000 was vast.

Then there were costs as well. So, in today's values, this was a significant fine but hardly an outrageous one. Nor was it one that Cotton could not easily afford to pay. However, no sooner was the verdict announced than that Toomey was on his feet, announcing that they would be appealing. Given the nature of his client, this was not altogether surprising. [3]

Appeal. Leinster Express 20. 10. 1883

Rev. S.G. Cotton's Appeal

The appeal was lodged by the Rev. S. G. Cotton, of Caragh Orphanage and Glebe, against the fine of £10 and costs imposed upon him by the magistrates sitting at Kilmeague petty sessions for cruelty to four of the orphan children under his charge at the orphanage, came before Dr. Darley, Q.C., Chairman of Quarter Sessions, at Naas, on Friday, 12 inst.

The following eight magistrates also occupied seats on the bench:

Lord Milltown, G. Tyrrell, Dr. Joly, Messrs T. Cooke Trench, W. Williams, B. Nicholson, H. Henry, and Fr. R. S. Hayes.

During the hearing of the case, the Courthouse was crowded, and most of the evidence was somewhat similar to that already adduced at the lower court.

─────────────────────────────

[3] The Irish Times- Saturday 15th September 1883

Mr Toomey appeared for the appellant and Mr Lord. S.C.S. represented the Crown authorities.

Mr Lord, in opening the case, said the appellant, the Rev. S.G. Cotton, had been summoned to the Kilmeague petty sessions for logging four of the orphans.

The summons was for an aggravated assault, and the magistrates convicted the appellant and fined him £10. In three cases, £2 each, and in the case of a little girl named Ellen Kelly, £4.

Of course, there was the usual alternative of imprisonment. The bench comprised two resident magistrates. He felt it to be his duty, having regard to the serious nature of the offence, to recommend that the appellant should be returned for trial before a jury, but the magistrates, inclined no doubt, to take a more lenient view of the case imposed the penalty already mentioned, in the hope that the matter would no more be heard of.

He was sorry to say the case had to be opened up again and that it would have to be commenced anew.

At the court below, Mr Toomey, who appeared for the Rev. gentleman contended that the punishment inflicted was perfectly legitimate, but he (Mr Lord) was sure the court would differ with the view when they heard the evidence. He did not see how they could possibly come to any other conclusion than that arrived at by the court below.

Rather the question would be whether that fine should not be increased. He had no doubt that the lower court's decision would be upheld.

Mr Toomey said there was nothing whatever in controversy between them. He produced the logs and chains, which were handed up to the bench, and admitted that they were used.

His worship stated that, notwithstanding the admissions made, it might be better to examine witnesses in order to make the bench acquainted with the facts.

It may be one thing to appeal against a fine, but what Cotton next did was totally inexplicable and made no sense other than that these were the actions of an incurable self-publicist and attention seeker. It has to be remembered that this case, of his being charged with cruelty to children by logging them, drew massive public attention. The courthouse was packed to capacity every day, and the press coverage was unprecedented. Every newspaper on both sides of the Irish Sea covered the Cotton story in varying detail. Some as leading articles, some as full-length features.

The Rev. Samuel G. Cotton, an obscure or little-known Church of Ireland country rector, was suddenly, overnight as it were, catapulted into national and international prominence. And while the reason for this notoriety was not particularly edifying and would make most rational people cringe, this was not how the Rev. Samuel saw things. No, he wallowed in his own infamy and would milk it for all it was worth.

We see an example of this mindset in The Irish Times of Saturday, September 15[th,] 1883, immediately following his conviction in Kilmeague, a letter to the editor penned by the Rev. Cotton. It reads as follows:

> *"Sir, I ask permission to remark that in your leading article of yesterday, you are not accurate in assuming that the boy who was logged was working in a field. He went into the field of his own choice."*

The letter continues in this self-serving manner where Cotton again tries to justify chaining children to each other and to logs. He even goes so far as to blame one of the victims – Ellen Kelly, for her own misfortune.

> *"The girl, a very bad and vicious character, was chiefly employed at her desk in school sewing and washing where the log was no inconvenience to her."*

This letter to the editor of The Irish Times is utterly pointless in terms of redeeming its author. What does it matter whether William Nolan was out in a field or up a tree? The fact of the matter remains that Cotton abused this young boy by chaining a log to his leg.

Something he does not deny being fair. But in publishing this drivel, the editor seems to give the Reverend gentleman more rope to hang himself with.

The appeal against the size of the fine was heard on October 12th, 1883, before the Naas Quarter Session and Dr. Darley Q.C. The following magistrates were on the bench: Earl of Milltown, Baron de Robeck, Messrs Williams, Tyrell, Nicholson, Dr. Joly, Thomas Cooke Trench, Hugh Henry, and W. A. Craig.

Defending the Kilmeague decision was again Crown Solicitor Mr E. Lord, and opposing that decision again was Mr Toomey appearing on behalf of the Rev. Cotton.

Again, a problem with this appeal is that it drew massive public attention. Word was out now that The Vicar of Caragh was capable of committing atrocious acts of cruelty against defenceless children. And while Cotton may have embraced bad publicity and even courted it, it cannot have done any favours to himself or his institution. The courtroom was packed to capacity, the newspapers full of it. The Vicar of Caragh was becoming infamous. Infamy he seemed not to care a jot about.

Most of what transpired during this appeal had already been heard in Kilmeague a month earlier. Head Constable O'Sullivan repeated his evidence in Kilmeague, only this time adding that when he came across John Ross and John Cleary chained together, and one of them chained to a log, they were on their knees on the gravel picking grass, weeding in other words.

Ellen Kelly appeared in the witness box and confirmed that she had been logged for nine days and nine nights that she had to do the work of the orphanage while so tethered and was required to sleep with the log chained to her ankle.

Ellen also confirmed that a year and a half earlier, the Rev. Mr Cotton had found her a situation working for a Mrs Hannon, wife of the Rev. Hannon, in Drogheda. However, this position was short-lived because she was made to appear before the magistrate court charged with attempting to burn the house down.

Following this, she was returned to the Caragh Orphanage. She also confirmed that she was flogged by Mr Cotton.

At the conclusion of this appeal, the magistrates were divided as to the correctness of the fine handed down in Kilmeague, referred to as "the court below", a month earlier. Four of these gentlemen were for upholding the decision of the court below, while five of them thought that the fine should be reduced by half.

One of those in favour of leaving the fine stand as was handed down was the chairman, His Honour Dr. Darley Q.C. He pointed out to the others that, as a general rule, appeal tribunals did not disturb the decision of the court below unless they were of the opinion that that court was wrong. And it was Dr. Darley's opinion that the court was not wrong and that the fine should remain unchanged.

Lord Milltown agreed with this, as did Thomas Cooke Trench, who described Cotton's behaviour in logging Ellen Kelly for nine days as "one of the most revolting nature, contrary to all the feelings of all humanity". However, the majority opinion had to prevail in law and Cotton's fine was halved and reduced to £5.00.

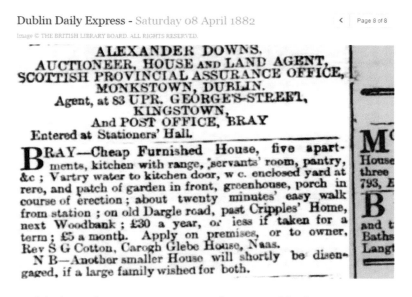

ALEXANDER DOWNS,
AUCTIONEER, HOUSE AND LAND AGENT,
SCOTTISH PROVINCIAL ASSURANCE OFFICE,
MONKSTOWN, DUBLIN.
Agent, at 83 UPR. GEORGE'S-STREET,
KINGSTOWN,
And POST OFFICE, BRAY
Entered at Stationers' Hall.

BRAY—Cheap Furnished House, five apartments, kitchen with range, servants' room, pantry, &c ; Vartry water to kitchen door, w c. enclosed yard at rere, and patch of garden in front, greenhouse, porch in course of erection ; about twenty minutes' easy walk from station ; on old Dargle road, past Cripples' Home, next Woodbank ; £30 a year, or less if taken for a term ; £5 a month. Apply on premises, or to owner, Rev S G Cotton, Carogh Glebe House, Naas.
N B—Another smaller House will shortly be disengaged, if a large family wished for both.

This shows that Cotton was a man of means and in the property business.

The editorial in the Leinster Leader the following Saturday, October 20th, 1883, did not pull any punches:

"The Rev. Mr Cotton has small reason to feel satisfied with the results of his appeal, and friends of humanity have cause to rejoice that

the barbarous ill-treatment inflicted upon helpless children in the notorious institution which the Rev. Evangelizer manages has been further exposed and more decisively condemned. True, the penalty was reduced somewhat, but the moral effect of the whole proceeding is to emphasise the verdict of the Magistrates who sentenced Mr Cotton to a fine of £10 at Kilmeague Petty Sessions. Of the manner in which the reduction of the penalty was accomplished, we can hardly trust ourselves to speak. It is not calculated to inspire people with a high sense of the judicial qualities of the 'great unpaid' to witness Justices of the Peace whipped in from the most distant parts of the county to sit on a Bench, where they were never seen before, for the purpose of whitewashing an institution which has been proved in open court to having been managed on the principles that immortalised 'Do-the-Boys Hall', and with the further object of licensing this latter day Squires to still pursue his humane methods of spanceling and logging. We should have thought that even bigots would not mingle inhumanity with their bigotry; it might have been expected that a sense of shame would have deterred gentlemen from combining to bolster up the system of evangelising which consists of buying into utter slavery infants at so much a head, and of instilling into their souls a knowledge of Him who loves little children by a course of savage punishment."

Shortly after this case, Cotton decided to dump Ellen Kelly at the gates of the poor house in Naas. This, of course, drew a strong reaction with those in charge of the poor house refusing to take Ellen under their care, saying that she was Cotton's responsibility. A row ensued, and Cotton simply walked away, leaving Ellen to her own faith.

Soon after this, we find her working at a linen manufacturer in Lisburn and trying to make a new life for herself. Mr Sinton, the owner of the Linen Company, has received, on two occasions, letters from Cotton asking if the girl was still in his employment. Then he asks if the girl had been pregnant and charged with infanticide in Northern Ireland.

Miss Sinton replied to Mr Cotton, stating that the young girl Ellen was indeed in her father's employment and was of very good character. She added that she had never been in trouble or ever prosecuted on any charge. Mr Cotton, not content with the reply, wrote again and sent four police officers to the factory door. Here they were asking if she had had a baby and killed it.

Mr Sinton thought he knew Cotton, but he had not heard that Ellen had been dumped in the Poor House days before coming into his employment. He was shocked and wondered about the appropriateness of a young girl being in Cotton's care.

He declared:

"The language which Mr Cotton described this girl is such never heard from the mouth of a gentleman and how he endeavoured to defame the character of a poor orphan and drive her to form trying to build a life for herself and her new job in which she is honestly earning her bread."

Mr Sinton hoped that some steps would be taken to hold Rev. Mr Cotton accountable for his conduct and that a grave duty lies on the patrons of the Caragh Orphanage. Mr Cotton ought not to be continued in his position for a day or an hour longer. Logging and changing defenceless and powerless little children were criminal, and surely once a child has been set free beyond the wall of Caragh, if, she may not hope for the help or sympathy of her former carer, she might at least expect to be safe from Mr Cotton and his defamations.

It seems that by his failed attempt to slander Ellen's good name with the most disgusting and untrue accusations, including that of child murder, Cotton was attempting to discredit her and make her an 'unreliable' witness in the event of her ever-giving evidence against him. That she had secrets Cotton wanted to be silenced is inescapable.

6 - Cruelty to children. Evacuation of the orphanage. Arrest and remanded in prison.

The portrait is that of the Rev. Samuel George Cotton, charged with illtreating and neglecting five children at Carogh Orphanage, County Kildare.

Rev. John Watson, Rector of Charlemont, near Moy, Co. Armagh, was a very worried man. Having the responsibility for the care of seven children from the same family cast upon him, this was proving disastrous. He was responsible for the safekeeping of the Burnett children, aged between 9 months and 16 years[4], all born out of wedlock. Their mother had died after the birth of her seventh child, and they were now in a state of destitution.

The children were Annie (16), Alexander (12), James (9), Samuel (8), Minnie (4), Elizabeth (3), and Mary (1m). Out of pure Christian kindness, Rev. Watson had taken it upon himself to have these children cared for in some institute designed for that purpose. Having made exhaustive enquiries, he had failed to find anywhere suitable to place the children. Nobody wanted them because they were illegitimate and without any means of support. Someone had suggested the Caragh Orphanage to him, and to his great relief, Rev. Cotton seemed willing to take the children under his care. Accordingly, the Burnett children were sent to Caragh.

---

[4] Annie, born 17 Jun 1874 / Alexander, born 19 Feb 1879 / James, born 6 Jun 1881 / Samuel, born 27 Apr 1883 / Mary (Minnie) born 25 May 1886 / Elizabeth, born 15 Feb 1888 / Mary, born 11 Dec 1890. Except for the eldest child, the name of the father is registered as Robert Burnett, labourer, and the mother as Mary Burnett, formerly Moffat. Subsequently, on 19 Aug 1891, Bridget McCusker, who had been present for four of the births, made a statutory declaration stating that the parents were not legally married, and this was noted retrospectively.

All was well for a few months, with Watson paying Cotton regular sums of money towards the children's upkeep in exchange for Cotton providing him with glowing reports as to how well they were doing.

In June, Rev. Cotton complained that he would have to return the children if he did not receive more money for their support. On 30th June, he wrote to Rev. Watson that he required between £60 and £70 for each of them, as he was £250 out of pocket, and if people who were interested in their welfare did not "liberally respond", he would have to send them back.

This is when things begin to go seriously wrong for Cotton and his quasi-orphanage. The Rev. Watson and the little girl Lizzy Burnett were about to, unknowingly, of course at the time, start a process that was to end it all very quickly. The horrors behind the walls of the orphanage are about to be exposed for all to see.

Not surprisingly, things were far from Cotton's reporting of them to Watson. On 28th July 1891, it had come to Rev. Watson's attention that the youngest child, 3-year-old Lizzy, had been admitted to the

Adelaide Hospital in Dublin with gangrene of all toes of both feet. This resulted from gross and prolonged neglect, hunger, and exposure to frost. The terrible state in which she arrived at the Adelaide was later described by Miss Knight, the Matron:

"She received Elizabeth Burnett from Rev. Cotton on 29th April 1891. Her clothes were sound and warm but reeking with filth and vermin. They had to be burned. Her hair was also full of vermin and had to be shaved, and her body was covered with parasites. Her feet were in a dreadful condition, wrapped in dirty rags, with her toes black and dropping off. Dr. Bamby, one of the medical staff at the hospital, saw Elizabeth the morning she was admitted and noted that she was exceedingly thin, her ribs sticking out, appearing malnourished, and she took food ravenously. He noted that some of her toes fell off subsequently, and others he had to cut off when they deteriorated."

Alarmed by this terrible news, Rev. Watson decided he had better make an unannounced visit to the Caragh Orphanage. The events which followed were first outlined at the Robertstown Petty Sessions court on 27th October 1891, the Cotton's having been summoned by the Irish Society for the Prevention of Cruelty to Children as a result of the conditions observed by Rev. Watson and reported by him to the Society. These events were as follows, and they are truly shocking.

On 14th October 1891, Rev. Watson visited the orphanage with two inspectors of the Irish Society for the Prevention of Cruelty to Children (ISPCC), Francis Murphy and James Dowsett. After having some difficulty in gaining admission, they entered the kitchen, being met at the door by James, Samuel, and Mary Burnett, whom Rev. Watson did not recognise, so changed was their appearance until they spoke. They pleaded with Watson to take them out of there.

They then visited the schoolroom, where some children presented a miserable appearance. The bedrooms were in a filthy state. One of the iron beds had no bedding. Another bench had on it what seemed to be a sack stuffed with hay. The coverings on the beds were abominable. The hay was filthy. In the corner of the room, they observed something moving, an infant of the most sickening appearance, the hay being damp, as were the clothes and floor beneath it. Another infant was found lying nearby, lying in its own filth, and the steam rising from the hay beneath it was most sickening and made him ill for two hours afterwards. In the bathroom, all the panes of glass in the windows were broken, and the bath was rusty and full of filthy water.

They next saw Mrs Cotton at the Glebe House and told her how they had found matters. She said Mr Cotton had been away, and the matron had neglected to do her duty. They then returned to the orphanage, where Mrs Cotton complained of the state of the place, to which the matron replied that she had neither coal nor clothes to warm the children. She asked Mrs Cotton if she should clothe the children in their Sunday clothes, to which Mrs Cotton replied "No". Rev. Watson said that the Sunday clothes were all for one purpose: to deceive the public. He then removed Alexander Burnett, the eldest child (age 13), whose head and body were in a filthy state, and brought him to the South Dublin Union Workhouse.

The following day, 15th October, Rev. Watson returned to Caragh with the two inspectors from the ISPCC, Mr Dowsett and Mr Murphy, and the Society's Doctor, John McVeigh. In later evidence given in court, Dr. McVeigh stated that he found the rooms in a most filthy condition and a little infant in the kitchen. His name was Thomas Collins, aged about 6 weeks, whose body was clothed with dirty rags and was evidently dying from cold and malnutrition, as stated by Dr. McVeigh. Another child, aged about 3 months, was also in a filthy state. A third infant, aged about 9 months, was badly clad and dirty. Ellen Carson, aged 2 years, was in a similar state. Patience Walker, Henry Norton & Eliza Winter, aged 4 years, Charles Quillet, Thomas Whitney, and Thomas Warren, aged 5 years, and Benjamin Wallace, aged 6 years, were all in a most wretched state from improper food, clothing, and want of cleanliness.

The limbs of the children were emaciated and their bodies anaemic. Their growth was stunted, and they had no appearance of muscular activity or development. Several had blisters. The house's sanitary condition and surroundings were the most appalling thing he had ever witnessed. The floors were filthy, and the walls were in a similar state. The bedrooms were wretched, with the window panes broken, there was no fire, the beds were filthy, covered with stale hay, and the air was foul all through the house. All the children were shivering from the cold and apparently in a state of terror.

The kitchen was in a most dilapidated state, with a small fire around which a few children were trying to warm themselves. In the yard outside, everything was in a fearful condition. The force pump, which supplied the inmates with water, was embedded in a mass of gutter and ordure, while the other sanitary arrangements were in a most shocking condition.

Rev. Watson took away the Burnett children, and they were lodged in Mrs Carr's home in Dublin. Within a week, Rev. Cotton, who had returned from England on 20th October, following an absence of 6 weeks, was summoned by the ISPCC for cruelty to children in his charge.

It would appear that Rev. Watson had recommended the Caragh Orphanage to the

Archbishop of Armagh during Rev. Cotton's visit to the diocese in July 1891. A letter appeared in local papers signed by the archbishop asking for public support for the orphanage. No doubt, it was a source of great embarrassment to Rev. Watson to have to inform the archbishop of the horrors he witnessed on his visit to Caragh. The archbishop wrote to Mr Cooke, secretary to the ISPCC, expressing his shock and disgust at what he had been told and requesting that his letter be published.

"The Palace, Armagh
Oct. 24

Dear Mr Cooke,

Some weeks ago, the Rev. Mr Cotton called on me, and from his plausible manner and gross misrepresentations, I was misled to recommend the Caragh Orphanage to public sympathy. From accurate inquiries and the statement of parties who have visited it, I unhesitatingly state that I believe it is a disgrace to our common humanity, the children fearfully neglected. I greatly fear, cruelly treated – in short, a public scandal. I hope that the Irish Society for the Prevention of Cruelty to Children will take up the case and prosecute the perpetrators. You may give any publicity to this letter to correct the effect of my

recommendation, procured by misstatements. I should
like if the case is tried, my letter to be read and published.

Yours truly,
Robert Armagh, Primate"

It was this letter that almost collapsed the trial of Cotton. It was claimed by the defence to be strongly prejudicial against an impartial hearing.

Robertstown Petty Sections, Tue. 27ᵗʰ Oct. 1891

The case was heard before Colonel Forbes at Robertstown Petty Sessions on Tuesday, 27ᵗʰ of October. The Cottons appeared in court with several of the children. The Society brought summonses for wilful neglect, mistreatment, and cruelty to the following children under their care: Alexander Burnett (13), Benjamin Wallace (6), Thomas Whitney (5), Thomas Warren (5), Henry Norton (4), Patience Walker (4), Elizabeth Winter (4), James Burnett (10), Samuel Burnett (8), Minnie Burnett (5), Elizabeth Burnett (3), Charles Quillet (2), Ellen Carson (2), Mary

Hurley (3 months) and Thomas Collins (3 months). The latter two were the victims of abandonment.

The case excited great interest in the general public. The Society's inspectors and doctors (Murphy, Dowsett, and McVeigh) all gave evidence describing the terrible state of the children and the conditions in the orphanage. It was noted that the case originated when Rev. Cotton brought Elizabeth Burnett to the Adelaide Hospital on 29th April 1891 suffering from gangrene of the feet, and the matron of the Adelaide gave evidence that the child was reeking with filth and dirt, so much so that her clothes had to be burned. She was swarming with vermin, and her head had to be shaved. Her toes were black and diseased on both feet, and she subsequently lost all of them. The doctor in attendance stated that she must have been in this condition for at least a week and was grossly neglected. She was also ravenous for food.

Dr. Cherry, for the prosecution, offered to show the magistrates Elizabeth Burnett's feet, as she was in attendance at court, but they declined. Mr Lanphier, for the defence, also objected to the showing of a sketch of her feet. Dr. Bewley, of the medical staff at the Adelaide, stated that Elizabeth was exceedingly thin, and her ribs were sticking out. He was of the opinion that she had not a sufficient supply of food to keep her healthy. Her weak physical condition probably exacerbated the gangrene of her toes. He saw her the day following her admission, but since then, some of her toes had fallen off, and others he had cut off with scissors when they became loose. The child had returned to perfect health but was still in the care of the hospital.

Rev. Watson, Rector of Charlemont, Co. Armagh, was then deposed. He states that he first sent Elizabeth Burnett to Rev. Cotton's orphanage at the beginning of January 1891 and that she was then in perfect health. In July, he was informed of her admission to the Adelaide Hospital. He made inquiries regarding the other Burnett children, informed by Rev. Cotton that they were all doing well. Knowing this to be a lie, Rev. Watson then arranged with the ISPCC to make an unannounced visit to the orphanage on October 14th, the details of which are related above.

Col. Forbes then declared that the bench was satisfied that a prima facie case had been made regarding Elizabeth Burnett and that he would return the case for trial at the assizes. Mr Lanphier requested the charges against Mrs Cotton be withdrawn, but the bench declined.

The charges concerning the other children were then dealt with. Rev. Watson gave details of his visit to the orphanage on the 14th of October and the terrible conditions he had encountered there. He described his conversation with Mrs Cotton in which she claimed the matron (Miss Hannen) had been neglecting her duties and Miss Hannen's statement that she had neither coal to burn nor clothes to put on the children. Dr. McVeigh was then deposed, stating that he was a medical officer to the Society, and he described in vivid detail the conditions he encountered on his visit there on 15th October, particularly the poor state of health of the children. Their growth was stunted, they had no appearance of muscular activity or development, were anaemic, and several were blistered. The sanitary conditions of the orphanage and its surroundings were the most appalling he had ever witnessed.

The bench then referred this second charge to the next assizes and consented to accept bail in two sureties of £25 each, and Rev. Cotton's own security of £50, and the same for Mrs Cotton.

Hercules Henry Dickinson, Dean of the Chapel Royal, who managed an orphanage in Dublin, wrote to the papers offering assistance in providing suitable accommodation for the children still remaining at Caragh and undertook to fundraise for that purpose. The ISPCC, still in its infancy, had no shelter for the reception of the children nor sufficient funds to support their placing in another home were grateful for the support offered by Dean Dickinson. The only caveat was that the children should be placed in a Protestant home, as was required by the Act of Parliament. Within days Dean Dickinson had received subscriptions of £135, which made possible the relocation of the younger children to Dublin on 4th November.

7 - Evacuation of Orphanage and Manslaughter Charge

A warrant signed by Major Forbes, R.M. on behalf of the ISPCC was executed on this day (4th Nov), and fourteen children, all under the age of 14, were removed from the orphanage to temporary accommodation in Dublin. Two inspectors from the Society and two nurses for the Adelaide Hospital were responsible for this action and were employed for this purpose by Dean Dickinson. But for warm wraps provided by him, the children would have been almost naked. They were placed the same evening in the Orthopaedic Hospital, Brunswick Street, as pay patients, a spare ward being provided for their reception. Five children remained at the orphanage because their names were not yet supplied to the inspectors by the Society and could not be included on the warrant.

On Saturday, 7th November, having obtained a new warrant from Col. Forbes for the remaining children, an official of the Society and two volunteers (Mr Harold Dickinson, son of Dean Dickinson, and Mr Gerald Colley), as well as a doctor and Mrs Meredith, Matron of St. Anne's Home, Dublin, who intended to take charge of the younger children, drove to the orphanage. One boy was delivered up, whom Rev. Cotton had claimed to be too ill to travel, but this was found to be false, and three others could not be found, having allegedly been sent to County Wicklow. Another child, over fourteen years of age and not included in the warrant, pleaded to be taken away, and both he and the younger boy were then driven to Naas station.

Rev. Cotton, on discovering the older boy was missing, followed in haste, reaching them at the station. He summoned Sergeant Nolan, then present, and told him the older boy had been illegally removed from the orphanage without a warrant. A large crowd gathered, surrounding the cab, and prevented Rev. Cotton from reaching the boy. Sergeant Nolan declined to interfere. The head constable was sent for, and the crowd, growing larger, jeered. By the time the train arrived, the crowd was in a 'dangerous state of excitement', and they prevented Rev. Cotton from interfering with the removal of the children from the cab to the train. As it left the station amid the loud cheers of the crowd, Rev. Cotton vowed to resort to legal proceedings.[5]

The children were brought to Dublin and placed in Dr. Steeven's Hospital. Dean Dickinson related that on returning from Dr. Steeven's Hospital, he found a letter on his hall table from a curate in one of the neighbouring city parishes mentioning that, in the course of his pastoral rounds on Saturday afternoon (7th Nov), he found three children from the Caragh Orphanage in a house in that parish. He was informed that Rev. Cotton was coming that night to take them away to another location. At once, Dean Dickinson, accompanied by his son and Mrs Meredith, went to Dublin Castle, and obtained the aid of two detectives and two uniformed policemen who proceeded to the address in order to take away the children, the warrant for whom Rev. Cotton had evaded. They found them hidden in a squalid attic in the house described in the letter. They were in a pitiable condition, one of them emaciated and his legs covered with ulcers, and all three in a most filthy state and covered with vermin.

---

[5] Freeman's Journal, Mon. 9 Nov 1891

They were removed to Dr. Steeven's Hospital and safely lodged there.

Cotton arrested in Dublin

On Monday, 9th November, Rev. Cotton was arrested in Parliament Street on a warrant issued by Col. Forbes at the instance of District Inspector Supple (Robertstown) and charged with the manslaughter of one William Brown some eleven years previously.[6]

He was taken to the Detective office in Exchange Court and shortly after removed to Kingsbridge Station and put on the 6:22pm train to Newbridge in the custody of D.I. Supple and, on arrival there, conveyed by car to the Curragh and brought before Col. Forbes. The depositions were read to the prisoner, and he was then remanded to Kilkenny Jail, bail being refused. Rev. Cotton was not represented. The following morning, he was conveyed to Kildare station en route

---

[6] On hearing of the news surrounding Caragh orphanage two former inmates, James Walsh, and William Goff, came forward to state that, about the year 1880, William Brown had died of exposure at the hands of Rev. Cotton, who, they claimed, had covered up his death to avoid an inquest.

to Kilkenny, to be held there till his next appearance at the Curragh special sessions the following Saturday.

Douglas arrested in Enniscorthy

On the same day, Monday, Mrs Margaret Douglas, née Condell, formerly matron of the Caragh Orphanage, was arrested in St. John's Terrace, Enniscorthy, charged with complicity in the alleged manslaughter of William Brown. The warrant had been signed by Col. Forbes at the same time as that for Rev. Cotton. The following evening, she was brought before Col. Forbes at Newbridge RIC barracks, and after depositions had been read to her, she was remanded to Grangegorman until the following Saturday sessions at the Curragh.

So now we have the situation where Cotton, out on bail for the charge of cruelty to children and awaiting trial for that, is arrested on the more serious charge of manslaughter. He is held as a remand prisoner in Kilkenny Goal.

Curragh Petty Sessions, Sat. 14th Nov. 1891

On Saturday, 14th November, Rev. Cotton was brought before Col. Forbes at the Curragh Petty Sessions and formally charged with the manslaughter of William Brown, aged 8 years, at the Caragh Orphanage on 7th December 1879. Several witnesses, former inmates of the orphanage, gave evidence of the events which led to the death of Brown.

Joseph Cuffe, aged 23, a former inmate of Caragh Orphanage and now a tram conductor, described as a smart, well-dressed young man, stated that he remembered the winter in question, which was a hard one. That morning another boy named Henry Thompson, who had been sleeping next to Brown, called out, "Oh Joe, I think Willie Brown is dead!" Brown had been sleeping on the floor, practically naked and covered only with a damp sack. This was not unusual, as Brown had been made to sleep on the floor as punishment for wetting his bed. This night had been particularly cold. Cuffe approached the child to find him dead, with the sack damp and stinking and frozen to Brown's body. He informed the matron, who sent him to the Glebe House to summon Rev. Cotton, who came down to the orphanage in an excited state. The body was put to bed, cold and stiff. Other boys present in the dormitory, according to Cuffe, were James Walsh (otherwise Wilmot), Joseph Clarke, Peter Gibbons, Joseph Murphy (otherwise Dyer), George Skerritt, and George Boyd.

James Walsh (otherwise Wilmot, aged 22) was next sworn and stated that the night Brown died was very cold, and there was snow on the ground. He thought Brown was weak and sickly, he had no boots, and his feet were always cold and blue with chilblains. The night before he died, he was given a cold bath, so cold in fact that the water had frozen and the ice had to be broken beforehand. He said Rev. Cotton ordered that any child who misbehaved was to be bathed and put to sleep on the floor. Thompson got the same treatment. Their supper was stopped, and they were made to sleep under a broken window, naked with only a sack for covering. The next morning Brown was dead.

James Walsh also stated that it was the custom of Rev. Cotton to alter the surnames of the boys, and he believed that his real name was Wilmot. He also named the boys who were present in the dormitory that night, and the names were the same as given by Joseph Cuffe, with the addition of Thomas Nolan.

Mrs Margaret Douglas (née Condell) was next sworn[7] in and stated that she first went to the orphanage in 1870 as a schoolteacher but also used to superintend the cooking and housework. She remembered Willie Brown. He had been an inmate of the orphanage since he was a baby. He was put out to nurse when he arrived from the Rotunda Hospital and returned when he was three or four years old. Because he used to wet his bed at night, he was punished by Rev. Cotton, who beat him with a cane or a thorny branch taken from the hedge nearby. She saw Brown's back bleeding from these beatings. He was not allowed to sleep in a bed like the other boys but had to sleep on the bare floor on some straw, without a nightshirt and only a sack for cover.

---

[7] Mrs Douglas was the lady arrested in Enniscorthy on 9th November, the same day as Rev. Cotton was arrested in Dublin.

When Dr. Sale saw the boys, he ordered all to be given bread and milk, but Rev. Cotton would not allow Brown any milk, and Mrs Douglas further stated that Mr Cotton used to beat Brown once a day, and she was under strict orders not to allow him to sleep in a bed. After discovering Brown had died, Dr. Sale was sent for, and when he left, Rev. Cotton stated to two of the boys that it was a good thing that Dr. Sale saw no need for an inquest, as it would be a "troublesome affair". Dr. Sale, according to Mrs Douglas, used to attend the orphanage about once a fortnight but never attended Brown except for the complaint of bed-wetting and had recommended for him bread and milk. Other than this, Brown was never a day sick.

Joseph Clarke, aged 19, a printer in Dublin, was next sworn. He remembered Willie Brown as a healthy-looking boy. However, he was more cruelly treated by Rev. Cotton and beaten with a cane about the head and body. On discovering Brown had died, he heard Cotton say regarding an inquest that it would "not look well to have a Papist jury".

Peter Gibbons, ex-Caragh Orphanage but by now a farm labourer, was next sworn. He remembered the night Brown died. He saw him after his bath, lying on the floorboards. He was crying from the cold. He had no bedclothes on him, only a sack. Gibbons stated that he did not see Brown beaten, only a few slaps from the schoolmistress.

At this point, the case was adjourned until the following Friday, 20th November, and Rev. Cotton was admitted to bail in the amount of £1,000 of his own accord and one surety of £1,000. At the time, this was a massive security payment away beyond the means of most people of the time.

Curragh Petty Sessions, Fri. 20th Nov. 1891

The case resumed before Col. Forbes at the Curragh the following Friday, and Joseph Dyer of Edinburgh gave evidence. He corroborated much of the evidence given by the other boys, adding that he used to notice Brown's feet bleeding after his bath due to (he thought) coming in contact with ice in the water. When asked his opinion as to the cause of death, he stated that he thought he died of cold and hunger.

D.I. Supple was next examined. He produced a death certificate for Brown stating the cause of death to be "cerebrospinal meningitis" of duration 2 days (uncertified). The date of death was 7th December 1879, and the age of the deceased was 6 years.

This death certificate was entered into the record and is taken from that provided by Dr. Sale.

Robert Jackson, Surgeon Captain of the Medical Staff at the Curragh Camp, was examined as to the probability of the reason given for death is accurate, and he stated that in his opinion, it was not, but that Brown probably died from cold and exposure, exacerbated by the low-quality diet he received at the orphanage.

In summing up the case for the defence Dr. Falconer, counsel for Cotton, produced no evidence in support of his client but declared that discrepancies in the dates given by the witnesses meant that they must refer to another boy and not Brown, but this was discounted by counsel for the prosecution (Mr White) who claimed that the witnesses were very young when Brown died (12 years previously) and could not possibly recall the dates with accuracy. Another point made by Dr. Falconer was that Rev. Cotton had no direct contact with Brown on the night of his death, but again this was discounted as it had been stated Rev. Cotton had beaten Brown with a thorny stick until he drew blood.

Col. Forbes said he felt bound to commit Rev. Cotton for trial at the next assizes. Bail was refused. Mr White then applied for Rev. Cotton to be remanded on a further charge of manslaughter, that of Thomas Collins, who died in the Orthopaedic Hospital, Dublin, on 11th November. This was the near-dead baby that the inspectors found, as described earlier.

He read the evidence made by D.I. Supple, setting forth the charge, and the verdict returned by the Coroner's Jury on 18th November. Col. Forbes granted the application. Rev. Cotton was then taken into custody and remanded on the second charge of manslaughter to the Robertstown Petty Sessions on Tuesday, 24th November.

Robertstown Petty Sessions, Tue. 24th Nov. 1891

Now we return to the charges of ill-treatment although, inadvertently, perhaps. Manslaughter charges are also touched upon.

At Robertstown Petty Sessions before Col. Forbes and Dr. Neale, Rev. Cotton and Mrs Cotton were charged with two summonses each of wilfully "illtreating, neglecting and exposing" Adelaide Parker, Kathleen Lynch, Annie King, Mary Wills (Willett), Bernard Savage, Thomas Brown, Charles Headley, and Robert Steele. The prosecution was at the suit of Francis Murphy, Inspector of the Irish Society for the Prevention of Cruelty to Children. Mr P. J. McCann, solicitor, represented the Society, and Dr. Falconer (instructed by W. A. Lanphier), defended.

Mr McCann explained that originally three of the named children (Mary Wills, Bernard Savage, and Thomas Brown) had not been included in the original prosecution as their names were not known, they are having been "spirited away" by Rev. Cotton and subsequently traced by the Society, with the assistance of Dean Dickinson, to an attic in Mercer Street, Dublin.

Evidence was given by Anne Burnett, who had been a servant to the Cottons at the Glebe House but was now living at Mrs Carr's home in Eccles Street, Dublin. She repeated the evidence given previously as to the conditions at the orphanage. Dr. McVeigh, a physician to the ISPCC and of Temple Street Children's Hospital, Dublin, deposed that he had visited the orphanage at the request of the Society on 15th October and noted that the sanitary conditions there were the most fearful he had ever seen.

The children were in a very weak, anaemic state. Their clothing was filthy, and their feet, legs, and toes were in a shocking diseased state. They were all stunted in growth for their ages. They were poorly dressed and had no shoes or stockings. He stated that he was a senior physician at the Children's Hospital and had more experience than anyone in children's diseases.

Francis Murphy, Inspector of the ISPCC, deposed that he had visited the orphanage on the 14th and 15th of October. He found the children dirty, underclad, miserable looking, and depressed. Their clothing was insufficient for the time of year and, in most cases, saturated with dirt. The sanitary conditions were very poor, the floors "simply abominable", the walls "begrimed with dirt". The mattresses were saturated with wet and dirt and emitted a very foul smell.

This closed the case for the prosecution.

For the defence, Dr. Falconer said that there was absolutely no evidence against Rev. Cotton. The charge of 'wilful' mistreatment of the children did not apply as Rev. Cotton was not present at the orphanage when the inspectors arrived, and, in any case, it was Miss

Hannen, the matron, who was responsible for the day-to-day running of the place.

The word "wilful" was to prove pivotal later, with the Carlow jury being unable to reach a unanimous verdict. The term actually served little purpose and only helped to confuse. The Cottons were very well aware of exactly what was going on in their hideous place. Allowing it to continue was wilful neglect. But perhaps it may have been too much to expect this subtility to be understood by all the "good men and true".

Col. Forbes stated that Rev. Cotton should be held legally responsible for what had occurred in the orphanage despite Dr. Falconer's claims to the contrary. Bail was refused for Rev. Cotton, but no objection was made to bail for Mrs Cotton. Dr. Falconer noted that nobody was prepared to offer bail for Rev. Cotton owing to the odium created by the newspapers. However, bail was accepted for Mrs Cotton in the amount of £50 of her own and one surety of £50. The charge of manslaughter of Thomas Collins was adjourned to the Curragh the following day, Wednesday, 25th November.

Col. Forbes presiding, the evidence given was practically a repetition of that given before the Coroner in Dublin on 12th and 18th November, in which the jury found that Thomas Collins died of pneumonia as a result of the poor treatment he received at the orphanage and that Rev. Cotton was responsible for that treatment. They had also condemned, in the strongest possible manner, the conduct of Mrs Cotton and regretted that the law did not allow them to include her in their verdict. William Grove-White, the Crown Solicitor, prosecuted, and Dr. Falconer (instructed by Mr Lanphier) appeared for the accused. Dr. McVeigh was first examined and stated that he had visited the orphanage on 15th October, where he saw the deceased child in a wretchedly miserable condition, almost a skeleton, and was of the opinion that he was dying from exposure, want of food, lack of cleanliness and general care. He did not think the child died from pneumonia.

He did not use the term "abandoned" because, as a means of killing babies, such a concept was not spoken of although widely practised.

Annie Burnett, a servant at the Glebe House, remembered Collins being brought to the orphanage, and a short time afterwards, he was a great deal worse than when he came. Emily Shelly, Lady Superintendent at the Orthopaedic Hospital, Dublin, deposed that she admitted the deceased and had never seen such a wretched child in her life. It was most emaciated and had no heat in its body. It weighed seven pounds. Adelaide Parker (13) stated that she was the child's nurse at the orphanage. He was not a very strong child when brought in by his mother and slept in hay on the floor, which was changed once a month. He had a quilt over him but no sheets or blankets. While she minded him, he got sores all over his legs and body. Shortly after his arrival Rev. Cotton went away.

Annie King (13) gave similar evidence. She said Collins slept in a box in the bedroom, with hay for bedding which was wet and insufficient. Adelaide Parker had charge of Collins, and she herself had charge of another baby, Minnie Burnett. It was also her business to prepare the beds, wash the clothes and clean the children's boots.

Col. Forbes said he would return the prisoner for trial at the Winter Assizes in Carlow on 9th December on two distinct charges of manslaughter (William Brown and Thomas Collins) and two separate charges of cruelty to inmates at the orphanage. Mrs Cotton would also be brought for trial at the Assizes.

Carlow Assizes, Wed. 9th Dec. 1891

The opening of the trial before Mr Justice Murphy was vividly described in the press:

"The trial of the Cottons began on Wednesday morning, 9th December. On the opening of the court, the benches and galleries were immediately filled, admission to the latter being by tickets from the High Sheriff. Nearly all the Protestant clergymen of the district were present, as were also some Catholic priests. There was a large sprinkling of ladies in the audience. The Crown decided to proceed with the charge of misdemeanour first, and under this charge, there were no less than forty counts

alleging cruelty and neglect on the part of the traversers towards the children at the orphanage. The Rev. Samuel Cotton, who had been in custody in Kilkenny Jail pending the trials, arrived by train in charge of warders and police. On entering the court, he was mobbed by a crowd, principally women and children, who denounced him heartily."[8]

The Solicitor General Q.C., Mr Ryan, Q.C., and Mr A. H. Ormsby, Q.C. (instructed by Mr W. G. White, Solicitor, Kildare) prosecuted. Mr Carson, Q.C., and Dr. Falconer (instructed by Mr Lanphier, Naas), defended.

Rev. John Watson was the first witness and described the horrific state of the orphanage when he visited with two inspectors of the ISPCC on 14th October. His testimony was the same as that given to the Robertstown and Curragh Petty Sessions. Mr Dowsett, one of the inspectors who accompanied Rev. Watson, corroborated his evidence as to the shocking conditions witnessed, as did Mr Murphy, the other inspector.

---

[8] The Nationalist, 10th December 1891

Further evidence was given by staff at the Adelaide and Dr. Steeven's Hospitals describing the terrible state of the children when admitted. Evidence given by Adelaide Parker (13) and the former matron Florence Hannen described Mrs Cotton as having been kind to the children, which was enough for the defence to request her acquittal on the grounds that no 'act of commission' could be proved against her.

Mr Justice Murphy agreed that there was no case against Mrs Cotton and that there was not a single act against her in respect of the charges made in this case. If a single act of violence or assault, the withholding of any article of food, or any changes injurious to the children were committed by her, then she would be liable, but none of these were the case. Things had gone on in the orphanage just as they had before her husband left for England, during which the ISPCC had visited and brought this case. He, therefore, directed her acquittal.

Eliza Cotton may not have committed any acts against any children. But she had to be fully aware of what was going on. By doing nothing then, surely, she was as guilty of neglect by omission as her husband was. But these were different times, and women were often acquitted in a manner that they would not be today.

Mr Carson, in his case for the defence, stated that he felt deeply at having to defend a minister of religion on charges revolting to all religions and that a verdict sending him to jail would be a small matter compared to his denunciation to the public as a traitor to the obligations which thirty or forty years previously he had undertaken when entering the Church. At his own discretion, he declined to call Rev. Cotton to the witness box but called Mrs Cotton instead. She stated she visited the orphanage almost every day, except recently, owing to the state of her health.

When asked could three girls aged 12 or 13 years nurse two delicate infants, three other infants, and five two-year-old children, she replied that this was done under the previous matron, Mrs Allen. Miss Hannen, who succeeded Mrs Allen, was dismissed by Rev. Cotton after Rev. Watson's visit and on the advice of Mrs Cotton, who claimed she had been neglecting her duty to care for the children. Mrs Cotton could not say that the children were crawling with vermin before she got sick. She said it was Miss Hannen's duty to report these things to her.

Dr. McVeigh, of the ISPCC, deposed that on 5th November, he had examined Thomas Warren (5) and Benjamin Wallace (6) and found their bodies marked with large contusions and welts, the result of a severe flogging about two weeks previously, and was told by the children that Rev. Cotton had beaten them. Thomas Hayne, one of the older boys, stated that he saw Rev. Cotton beat the two with his riding whip.

Summing up the case for the defence, Dr. Falconer hoped the jury would not be prejudiced by all they had heard in the newspapers. Mrs Cotton, of decent birth and accomplishments, had sacrificed her leisure to care "as tenderly as a mother could that miserable mite of diseased humanity, Thomas Collins, the offspring of sin and shame", as well as the other children. Mr Cotton had nothing to gain but conceived he was doing the master's work in saving the illegitimate children which no other institution would take, and was he to be held responsible if the father of the Burnett children was a diseased and dissipated scoundrel and their mother a prostitute? If the children were neglected, it was the fault of Miss Hannen and not of the Cottons.

Mr Ryan, Q.C., replied on behalf of the Crown. He stated that Rev. Cotton could not escape from the indictment on the grounds that he was absent, or that his wife was superintendent, or that his employee was also engaged to be criminally responsible for the neglect of her employers. The evidence was that the orphanage was found in a disgraceful condition. Should the accused be acquitted, it would delight the baby farmers of England and "render the law a dead letter".

The jury could not unanimously agree on a verdict and had questioned the meaning of "wilful neglect", and they were then discharged. The crux would seem to be on the word "wilful". Some of the jurors (probably just one) thought that the actions of the Cottons in neglecting the children, even to the point of death, were not wilful. This was at a time when a unanimous verdict was required by law. Just one dissenting juror could collapse a trial.

Mr Ryan, on behalf of the Crown, consented to the postponement of the two charges of manslaughter until the next Kildare assizes and to Mr Cotton being allowed out on bail. The judge agreed.

Queen's Bench, Sat., 20th Feb. 1892 Case moved to Belfast

Some weeks earlier, Mr Carson had applied, on behalf of Rev. Cotton, for an order to have the venue changed from Kildare to Dundalk, Longford, Belfast, or any other county the court might direct. This was because of the continuous bad press coverage and general hostility towards the Reverend.

After what Cotton had experienced by members of the general public, he believed he could not possibly get a fair trial in County Kildare, nor indeed in any of the adjoining counties. Mr Cotton's affidavit stated that during the first three days of his trial in Carlow, he would not be taken into any house in the town, and he had to travel to Athy in order to get food and lodgings.

On the last two days of the trial, he was admitted into one of the hotels in Carlow. But this was only after the police had threatened the proprietor with charges if he refused Cotton admission.

Since the trial in Carlow, he had been refused the necessities of life in the shops. Likewise, the men who went bail for him had been treated in the same way and shunned. When Cotton appeared in any town where there was any gathering of people, he was hooted and yelled at and subjected to insult and abuse.

Belfast Assizes, Day 1, Thur. 24 Mar 1892

In his book *The Trials of Edward Carson,* Marjoribanks gives us a good description of Cotton's demeanour in court.

REV. SAMUEL G. COTTON

First, the said reverend client's saint-like appearance and demeanour:

"There was a venerable clergyman, approaching the Psalmist's limit of human life, garbed in becoming clerical, and yet not offensively sacerdotal, cloths; his neck-tie was of the old voluminous innocent sort, tied in front in a rather awkward bow. No wonder the soft-hearted Kildare (sic) jury had disagreed! How could a shepherd, in his quest for money on behalf of the stray, orphan lambs, occupy himself with tying a neckcloth? He was pathetically deaf, so deaf that he was compelled to wear, attached to both ears, a little metal plate in the form of a concave shells that apparently served the purpose of a hearing trumpet."

When, in the course of the trial, a strong point was made against him, of course, he never heard - but one of his friends, a sort of interpreter of calumny, speaking into his ear, explained, or quoted, then followed an extra-clerical look of the resigned and forgiving Christian martyr on his pained but benign countenance.

The principal charge was again the wilful neglect and cruelty to the children in the Caragh Orphanage. But through some inexplicable clerical error, the charges of manslaughter were omitted in transferring the case from Carlow to Belfast. When the Crown tried to reintroduce manslaughter Carson would not allow this since it was not on the list of charges presented.

The courthouse was crowded, and a large number of fashionable ladies were present. Counsel for the Crown included the Solicitor General, J. H. Campbell, and W. P. Ball (instructed by Mr Grove White, Crown Solicitor for Kildare). The Defence was represented by Edward Carson, Q. C., and Dr. Falconer (instructed by Mr W. Lanphier of Naas).

Rev. John Watson was the first witness. He recalled writing to Rev. Cotton on 29th December 1890 in which he asked if he could send the Burnett children to Caragh, their mother having died following childbirth of her seventh baby. They would be in the company of their elder sister, Martha. Rev. Cotton accepted the children, and they were sent to him. On 11th July, Rev. Watson inquired how the children were doing and was informed by Rev. Cotton that they were happy and doing well.

However, at the end of July, Rev. Cotton wrote to Watson to tell him that Elizabeth Burnett was in hospital in Dublin. No further action was taken by Rev. Watson at this time as he was ill. On October 14th, however, some three months after being alerted, he visited the orphanage in the company of two inspectors of the ISPCC (Dowsett and Murphy).

This was the unannounced visit to the Caragh Orphanage, which was to lead to the ultimate downfall and ruin of Cotton. Following this visit, Watson instituted the present proceedings and removed the Burnett children from the orphanage.

Mr Dowsett, an inspector for the ISPCC, next took the witness stand. He had visited the orphanage on October 8th, 1891 but could not gain entry. The following week, accompanied by Rev. Watson and Francis Murphy, he revisited and was able to gain admission. He described seeing Mary Hurley, aged 3 months, looking very malnourished with vermin crawling about her face and neck. Her cotton clothing was wet and steaming. Thomas Collins looked like the perfect skeleton and was in a worse condition than Mary Hurley.

Francis Murphy, the inspector for the ISPCC, stated he found Collins in a filthy bed of hay from which emanated a sickening stench. His limbs were excoriated, and he was dressed in calico rags. Charles Quillett (aged 2 years) was also insufficiently clad, and his clothes were stiff with dirt.

Dr. McVeigh, medical officer for the ISPCC, described Patience Walker (aged 4 years) as suffering from ophthalmia (sore eyes). She had sores on her head and was covered with vermin. Charles Quillett had gangrene of the toes. He attributed their condition to neglect and malnutrition, which must have continued for at least a year.

Bertha Knight of the Adelaide Hospital described Elizabeth Burnett as emaciated, afflicted with vermin, and her toes were black, shrivelled, and dropping off. Dr. Henry Bewley, also of the Adelaide Hospital, described Elizabeth Burnett as exceedingly thin. Her ribs were sticking out. She ate ravenously, and the only sign of intelligence was when asked to have food. She later developed into a splendid little girl with proper food and care. Two of the Burnett children suffered from Reynaud's disease (Annie and Elizabeth).

Susan Beresford of the City of Dublin Hospital stated that Patience Walker was in poor condition on her admission and seized and devoured her food at first. She was subject to screaming fits. During her stay, she got strong and fat. Mrs Cotton visited her once.

Frances Meredith of St. Anne's Young Men's Home stated that she received Thomas Collins from the orphanage and conveyed him to the Orthopaedic Hospital. He had only three scraps of scanty clothing.

Emily Shelly, Lady Superintendent of the Orthopaedic Hospital, received Thomas Collins and thought he had no chance of living. Patience Walker could not stand the light when first brought in.

Dr. J. K. Denham, Medical Attendant at the Orthopaedic Hospital, weighed Thomas Collins at 7.25 lbs when he should have been closer to 18lbs for a child of his age. By order of the coroner, he did a post-mortem and found all his organs, except the lungs, to be healthy. The disease of the lungs was of recent origin. His emaciated condition he attributed to malnutrition. Mary Hurley seemed to be reasonably well-nourished. Patience Walker's head was badly broken out, caused by dirt and neglect.

This concluded the evidence of the first day.

Belfast Assizes, Day 2, Fri. March 25th, 1892

The trial continued the following morning, Friday, March 25th, and again the courthouse was crowded. There was a large attendance of ladies and numerous clergymen.

The evidence continued. Ellen Dunscombe of Dr. Steeven's Hospital described the condition of Charles Quillett. His clothes were filthy, he was very hungry, his stomach distended, and in her opinion, was unnaturally thin and malnourished. He was stated to be two years old, but she believed he was older, at least four years of age. He was in the hospital until January and improved every day.

Dr. Fergus, the Dispensary Doctor for Blackwater, Co. Armagh, stated that he knew the Burnett children before they were sent to the Caragh Orphanage. He examined Elizabeth Burnett on January 8th, 1891, and found her to be a strong, healthy child. When she was an infant, he had prescribed for her ophthalmia but did not examine her feet or head.

Adelaide Parker (aged 13) stated that she, Mary Mills, and Annie King had charge of the children. When Elizabeth Burnett arrived, there were 18 other children at the orphanage. Some of the bigger boys lived in the rectory. There were five infants. When Collins arrived, he was a fat child. There were seven beds in the girls' dormitories and four in the boys. Some slept on the floor. When Elizabeth came, she appeared in good health but took ill shortly afterwards. Mr Cotton visited the orphanage on Sundays and very occasionally during the week.

He did not go into the orphanage but saw them in the front garden or in the schoolroom on a wet day. He never visited the dormitories or examined the clothing or beds. Mrs Cotton visited the orphanage on Sundays and sometimes during the week. She never saw Mrs Cotton in the dormitories or examining the beds. Until Mr Watson's visit, Thomas Collins was never brought to the rectory. All the children, except the smaller ones, went to church on Sunday.

Miss Allen used to assist in cleaning the children, nursing the babies, and cooking the food, and she showed her how to cook the food and attend to the babies. She used to teach in the school, was kind to the children, and kept the rooms and beds clean. While she was in the orphanage, the children were well attended to.

Annie King (aged 13) stated that Thomas Collins was a healthy child when he arrived at the orphanage. When Miss Allen was there, the beds were dried at the fire. She used to look after the children and comb their hair. She was fond of them, and they liked her.

Florence Hannen, a former matron, stated that she went to the orphanage on July 3rd, 1891, and signed her contract on July 6th. Conditions at the orphanage were deplorable on her arrival. Mary Hurley was very sickly looking. Besides Thomas Collins, there were two other infants and one other child who could not walk. Collins was wretched when he arrived, and she did not see any change in him.

On October 24th, Rev. Cotton summoned her for ill-treating the babies. Miss Batterton was sent from Dublin to assist her but had "to be put away." Thomas

Collins and his mother arrived in a starved condition. Mr Cotton went away the day after Collins came and did not return until after the inspectors had been.

Anne Cleary, a former inmate, stated that she arrived in 1883 and stayed at the orphanage for five years. Miss Allen and Patience Walker were there then. Patience Walker arrived in 1887, and she noticed her condition. She had sores on her head, fingers, and feet.

This concluded on the second day of evidence.

Belfast Assizes, Day 3, Sat., March 26th, 1892

Much of the evidence gathered from here on in Belfast was a rehash of what had already taken place in Carlow. On Saturday morning, March 26th, the trial continued. As before, the courthouse was crowded with fashionable young ladies who remained in court during the adjournment for luncheon, nibbling biscuits, and buns, afraid they should lose their seats and any of the details of this 'nice' case.

Mrs Eliza Cotton took the witness box and was examined for four hours. She admitted that Lizzie Burnett looked healthy on her arrival, but her head was dirty. Her feet were noticed to have chilblains, and Dr. Sale was called. They were anointed with ointment and poulticed. Sometime later, he directed that she be taken to the Adelaide Hospital, which was carried out by Mr Cotton. Another of the Burnetts had sore fingers and was also sent to the same hospital and recovered. Dr. Sale thought she had the same disease as her sister.

Thomas Collins was a miserable child, a fortnight old, and looked starved. Mr Cotton left two days later. Miss Hannen refused to take charge of the baby because he was dying. Two weeks after Mr Cotton left, she caught a cold and had an attack of rheumatism. Adelaide Parker nursed baby Collins each day in her (Mrs Cotton's) room. He was fed on milk mixed with lime water and sugar and got as much as he required. The food did not seem to improve him. Patience Walker was a fine little girl but unhealthy when she arrived and had sore eyes. She was sent to Sandymount Convalescent Home for a month. Later she was taken to the City of Dublin Hospital by Mr

Cotton and visited by herself. And seemed bright and gay.

She did not see anything the matter with Mary Hurley when brought to the orphanage. Charles Quillett suffered from no disease but was always wanting food. He had worms, for which he was given medicine. On the day the inspectors came, he had fallen in the yard, and this accounted for his dirty clothes.

In September, Mr Cotton and herself thought Minnie Burnett, Mary Hurley, and Thomas Collins were not looking well. She told Miss Hannen she thought they were not getting all their milk. When she supervised their feeding, the children showed improvement.

After Mr Cotton left, she saw three little girls sleeping on the floor on hay with a blanket over them and said she could not allow that. Miss Hannen replied that "it was good enough for the little pigs".

Miss Allen was next examined. She stated that she was matron for 4 and a half years and left in July 1891.

She taught the children, assisted Mrs Cotton with the sewing, and superintended the cooking and cleaning of the children. In 1887 she was assisted by six girls, but in 1888 three left. The floors of the rooms and dormitories were washed every day. The beds and sheets were kept clean, and so were the children, each of whom had a change of clothing. All were properly kept and got as much stir-about as they desired.

The rest of her evidence went to show that the treatment of the children was good. On inquiry, she said she felt the Cottons had been hard used at the Carlow Assizes and had sent them a Christmas card and offered to give evidence in the case. Asked by the Solicitor General if she had been offered money by Mr Cotton to give such evidence, she replied that she could have gotten more money from the Crown if they had offered. The case was then adjourned until the following Monday.

This then would seem to suggest that she was bribed by Cotton to say all the right things.

Belfast Assizes, Day 4, Mon., March 28th, 1892

On Monday morning, March 28th, the courtroom was once again filled with fashionable and stylish-looking ladies, some with opera glasses. Many also brought their luncheons, fearful of losing their places if they left the courtroom. The evidence continued.

Thomas Nolan stated that he had worked at the Rectory but previously spent seven years in the orphanage. The rooms and beds were always kept clean in Miss Allen's time but were dirty on the day of Rev. Watson's visit. Eliza Tutty was a servant at the rectory for 2.5 years and corroborated the evidence given by Thomas Nolan. Cross-examined by the Solicitor General, she admitted that she had not visited the orphanage more than half a dozen times altogether.

Rev. Gibson, chaplain, and headmaster of the Bluecoat School made a report on February 26th, 1889, that all the children at the orphanage were clean and their progress in their studies satisfactory. The place was then kept clean. He had not visited the orphanage subsequently. Cross-examined, he said he was only with the children for one hour, and as far as he could see, they were clean.

Dr. Gregory Sale, physician, and surgeon for 20 years, examined by Mr Carson, stated that he had a dispensary a short distance from the orphanage (at Kilmeague). He gave his medical advice gratuitously. He examined Patience Walker, Elizabeth Burnett, and Thomas Collins after Rev. Watson's visit in October. Walker had scrofulous ophthalmia, which he considered hereditary and made her more prone to disease. Burnett was suffering from gangrene of the toes, and he directed her to be admitted to the hospital. Collins was suffering from a hereditary disease for which he prescribed an ointment and tonic, which would reduce his weight. He was always in Mrs Cotton's room, except on October 27th, when he was taken to the Petty Sessions Court. He improved after treatment and had colour on his face. He did not think it safe to take him on a long journey to Dublin, and everything was done for the child that was possible.

Counsel then read a letter written by Mr Cotton to Dr. Sale before Rev. Watson's visit and while he was in

London requesting him to go examine the orphanage and "if things were not right to give that little woman *[Miss Hannen]* a hearing". Cross-examined by Mr Campbell, he told him that following his visit to the orphanage on October 31st. He recommended the walls be whitewashed and that the youngest children should be removed as they did not look nearly as well as usual. He had originally given a certificate stating the orphanage to be in perfect order in 1880 and allowed Rev. Cotton to redate it in subsequent years. After Rev. Watson's visit, he refused to give a certificate. In 1882 he gave a certificate that the sewage works of the Glebe and orphanage were perfect in every way and would prevent sewage from getting access to the surface water or pump.

This closed the case for the defence.

In summing up, Dr. Falconer addressed the jury. He knew that in coming to Belfast, a fair trial would be had before a special jury of the Co. Antrim. This case, he asserted, first came to light because the head of the Irish Church did not approve of Rev. Cotton's preaching sermons in Presbyterian churches in Moy. The Crown had failed to produce any evidence as to the condition of the Burnett children when sent to the orphanage. He contended they could not have been clean and healthy when sent. It had been proved by Dr. Bewley that they suffered from Reynaud's disease, which was hereditary and caused the dropping off of the toes.

Note: Reynaud's Disease does not affect young children. It is not hereditary and does not cause toes to drop off. Frostbite does.

Patience Walker's scrofulous ophthalmia was the result of the sins of her father, and surely Rev. Cotton was not responsible for that. Worldly and cynical people would say that Rev. Cotton brought all this trouble upon himself by taking charge of little diseased children, but in taking Collins under his care, he probably saved the mother from the charge of child murder. How many men would allow their wives to nurse a child afflicted with a loathsome disease as Mr Cotton did? Collins died of pneumonia, contracted in the hospital in Dublin.

Mrs Cotton endeavoured to get an extra servant but was unable to do so because they were boycotted. Mr

Cotton could not be expected to attend to the babies as a nurse would. That was the duty of a woman. He could not anticipate in his absence Miss Hannen's dereliction of duty or his wife's illness. He could not be held liable for the state of the orphanage on October 14th.

The Solicitor General replied on behalf of the Crown. He commented on the fact that Mr Cotton had not dared go into the witness box to be questioned as his answers would have incriminated him. The defence was a cowardly one, namely throwing all the blame upon poor Miss Hannen, who was too good to be his underling. The jury would have to ask themselves whether the incompetent and insufficient staff and insufficient food were the cause of the neglect and ill-treatment found there. If the children suffered from hereditary disease, was that no reason why they should not have been more carefully looked after? The excuse that if he had not taken diseased Thomas Collins in, his mother would have drowned him in a pond and been hung for it, was lamentable.

It was all nonsense to say that the conditions found at the orphanage on October 14th arose in six weeks. Miss Hannen, a fragile little lady, was to "see to things". To see to what! To work miracles? That the staff existed? There were just three young girls to nurse all the babies, cook the food, work all day and then be ready at night to jump up whenever a baby cried. With regard to Patience Walker, it was strange that while in hospital, she grew fat and then became thin again in the orphanage. When sent to Mrs Smylie's home, she became well again and then returned to the orphanage to be found by the Society sitting by the fire crying with pain, the back of her head all sore and her body and clothes covered in vermin.

If Cotton knew she was suffering from a hereditary disease, he ought to have provided proper means for taking care of her, and if he did not, he was guilty of wilful neglect. It was said the Cottons were boycotted and could not get servants. The reason was that they would not pay proper wages. If Mrs Cotton was ill while her husband was away, she surely had the use of her pen and could have obtained someone who would have nursed Thomas Collins and properly attended him.

The Solicitor General then stated that the jury could come to no other conclusion other than the children had been neglected and ill-treated and that Mr Cotton knew of their condition.

Belfast Assizes, Day 5, Tue., March 29th, 1892

On Tuesday, March 29th, the Lord Chief Baron took one hour and forty minutes to sum up the case.

After a deliberation of an hour and a half, the jury came in with a verdict of guilty. Immediately Mr Carson was on his feet and made an hour and a half appeal to his lordship in mitigation of the punishment which might be inflicted. This, as it turned out, was to be a seminal moment in Carson's career. The speech got widespread publicly and brought public attention to Carson.

"I beseech you, your lordship, to consider the position of this old man. At the time of disestablishment (of the Church of England in Ireland), he even then advanced in life and sacrificed his own interests in order to promote the interests of

the religious body to which he belonged. In all the long period of his ministry, there was never a whisper that he was selfish, or avaricious, or careless of the sufferings of others. --- He started the orphanage. Who entering upon such a course could easily look forwards to ease and opulence, and, in heaven's name, who could think that any personal ends could be served by a systematic neglect of the orphans? ---- It is abundantly clear that my client is not a man of business and that he is weak, unpractical, prone to trust where he should suspect, and, for an old man, singularly, absurdly sanguine. Not the man, I admit, to manage an orphanage, but not of necessity a criminal. ---- Meanwhile, to obtain funds, this old man was compelled to be as constantly on the road as if he had been a commercial traveller. The orphanage saw very little of him: and while he toiled to collect funds, the working of the place devolved very much on others. ---- My client was very foolish, always hoping for some turn of luck: but I find it hard to consider him a mere vulgar criminal. I trust implicitly in your lordship's sense of fair play, your feelings of human sympathy, and perhaps I might venture to add of equity when you come to pass sentence on this broken old man."

This speech went on for an hour and a half. It was delivered in slow, measured tones to a hushed crowded courtroom. It has to be admitted that, given the nature of his client, Carson could hardly have done any more for him.

The case was adjourned until the following morning. The Crown Solicitor returned to Dublin in the afternoon to consult with the Solicitor General as to the other charges pending against the prisoner (felony charges of the manslaughter of William Brown and Thomas Collins). Rev. Cotton was released on his own bail of £2,000 and two sureties of £1,000. At the time, these were massive sums of money that yet again demonstrated that the Cottons were wealthy people. This money was accumulated from copious charitable donations. It was not used as it should have been on hiring proper professional staff, paying them accordingly, and minding the children properly.

Belfast Assizes, Day 6, Wed., March 30th, 1892

The following morning, Wednesday, March 30th, Rev. Cotton was brought before the Lord Chief Justice for sentencing, 'looking in a very anxious condition of mind'. Before sentencing, the Lord Chief Baron Palles asked the Crown prosecutors what was intended regarding the two felony charges of the manslaughter of William Brown and Thomas Collins. Mr Campbell, on behalf of the Crown, protested against the question of jurisdiction being raised by Mr Carson after the verdict had been reached.

The Crown would enter a *nolle prosequi* in the felony charges (manslaughter of Brown and Collins). His Lordship then decided to refer the question of jurisdiction to the Court for Crown Cases Reserved and to postpone sentencing until then. What this, in effect, meant was that the manslaughter charges would be put on hold for now.

The prisoner, in a faltering voice, agreed to be bound in the sum of £2,000 surety on condition that he surrender himself into the custody of the governor of her Majesty's prison at Belfast on the first day of the next Assizes of the County of Antrim and before the sitting of the Court on that day. Thomas Picton Reid of 5 Upper Temple Street, Dublin (Cotton's brother-in-law, a Solicitor) offered surety for the prisoner's appearance, and Rev. Cotton was then discharged and left the court in the company of several of his friends.

Court of Crown Cases Reserved, Thur., May 13th, 1892

In the meantime, in Dublin, five questions were considered:

- Firstly, whether the crimes included those in relation to Thomas Collins?
- Secondly, had the Antrim Grand Jury jurisdiction to inquire into the crimes mentioned in the order of the Queen's Bench, changing the place of trial to Belfast?
- Thirdly, whether the indictment ought to have been quashed by the Chief Baron?
- Fourthly, should judgement be arrested?
- Fifthly, what judgement should be given to the verdict?

After much legal consideration and arguments on both sides concerning the validity of the Queen's Bench order of February 27th, 1892 (in which the name of Thomas Collins was inadvertently omitted when changing the venue of the trial from Carlow to Belfast), the verdict of the court was reserved until the following week, Wednesday, May 18th. At the second sitting of the Court of Crown Cases reserved in Dublin, the nine justices each gave their considered legal opinion and were unanimous in deciding for the Crown the uphold the conviction of Cotton. The inadvertent omission of the name of Thomas Collins earlier was not a reason to cause the case to collapse, as he would have been included as one of the orphans in the general indictment where it specified - *and others.*

Belfast Assizes, Day 7, Sat., July 23rd, 1892

On Friday, July 22nd, Rev. Cotton surrendered to bail in Belfast and was removed to the County Jail. On the following morning, Saturday, July 23rd, Justice Holmes acting for Chief Baron Palles, sentenced him to six months imprisonment without hard labour and a fine of £400. The leniency of the sentence was due to his age. The prisoner appeared before the court with a bandage over one eye. He attempted to address the court to refer to medical reports sent to the Lord Chief Baron, which were acknowledged by Justice Holmes, and considered when passing judgement. Rev. Cotton then asked to be treated as a "first-class misdemeanant" but Justice Holmes said he had no power other than to carry out the sentence issued by the Lord Chief Baron. The prisoner was then removed into custody in Belfast that evening and transferred by train to Mountjoy Prison the following morning.

8 – Imprisonment and release from Mountjoy Jail

While in Mountjoy Prison, Cotton underwent regular medical examinations.

Here is a typical example of such a report written into his prison records. In it, we find that:

- In general, his health was good for his age.
- He suffered from glaucoma of both eyes.
- He suffered from inguinal hernia and haemorrhoids.
- His heart was irregular in rhythm.
- He had glycosuria or protein in his urine.

- His height was only 5 ft 4 ins.
- His life was not being endangered by imprisonment. "Let the law take its course" - was the consistent recommendation from the examining doctor.

These prison medical records are impressive. They are consistent. They show care and attention to detail. Diagnosing what was probably Atrial Fibrillation using only a stethoscope needed attention to detail and could easily have been missed.

In parallel to these prison doctor's reports, we also get ones from outside private doctors paid for by Cotton. They do not differ materially from the in-house ones other than they say continued imprisonment may shorten the prisoner's life.

Rev. Cotton, having served his six-month sentence, was released on Friday morning, January 27th, 1893, and proceeded to Naas on the 10.00 am train from Kingsbridge. He then drove immediately to Caragh. It was reported that he did not look the worse for wear after his time in Mountjoy prison but had lost the sight in one of his eyes, from which he had previously suffered. In a conversation with his solicitor, Mr Lanphier, he spoke highly of the prison officials, in particular, the governor and medical officer. He had spent three of his six-month sentences in hospital.[9] While in the prison hospital, he was allowed to take alcohol under the supervision and for "medicinal purposes only".

For a time, Cotton seems to have kept a low profile but came to the attention of the newspapers again on Monday, May 29th, 1893, when a notice was posted at Naas Town Hall advertising the auction by District Inspector Supple, on the following day, of goods seized from him for non-payment of the fine of £400 imposed on his conviction in Belfast the previous July.[10] The sale at Robertstown Barracks included two mares, a two-year-old filly, a foal, a milch cow, three calves, two pigs, a brougham, a spring van, two drays, four revolvers, a gold watch, and sundry other articles. There were also two life assurance policies on his own life in the sums of £150 and £200. Evidently, Rev.

---

[9] Irish Independent, Sat., 28th Jan. 1893 / Kilkenny Moderator, Wed. 1st Feb 1893
[10] Irish Independent, Tue. 30th May 1893

Cotton was concerned for his own welfare as it was most unusual for a man of the cloth to be so well armed. The goods were purchased by Mrs Cotton for the sum of £88.

9 – Reoffending and imprisonment Kilkenny Jail

In June, a question was raised in the House of Commons by Mr Horace Plunkett relating to an allegation that Rev. Cotton was again conducting an orphanage at Caragh. The reply was that the police who had ascertained two children were then at the orphanage and that when the officer asked to see them, he was directed by Rev. Cotton to leave the premises. The District Inspector was informed that, if necessary, a magistrate may issue a warrant, and if mistreatment of children was suspected, then proceedings could be taken.[11] There the matter rested until the following February.

On Tuesday, February 20th, 1894, acting on a warrant under the Prevention of Cruelty to Children Act, D.I. Supple proceeded with Head Constable McKeon, Sergeant Nolan, Acting Sergeant Synnott, Constables Donnelly and Mullally, and Dr. McDonagh to the Caragh Orphanage where they found two children sitting in the kitchen in a most emaciated

---

[11] Dublin Daily Express, Sat. 17 Jun 1893

condition, their feet covered with sores. Rev. Cotton was not at home, but Mrs Cotton was present. They took charge of the children and conveyed them to the workhouse in Naas, where they were photographed and weighed. The children were the only ones at the orphanage.

The following Tuesday, February 27th, at Robertstown Petty Sessions before Col. Forbes, Dr. Neale, and Mr Thornhill, J.P., Rev. Cotton was charged with cruelly, ill-treating the two children, whose names were Mary Dennison (aged 7) and her brother Thomas (aged 3). D.I. Supple prosecuted for the R.I.C. and Mr Stephen Brown appeared for the ISPCC.

Rev. Cotton asked for an adjournment of the case for one month as his counsel, Dr. Falconer, was unavoidably detained at the Nenagh Petty Sessions and would be tied up for a further three weeks. The Crown objected, but on further consultation with Col. Forbes, it was agreed that the case is adjourned for one week, with Rev. Cotton paying expenses of two guineas. Mrs Cotton then wrote a cheque for this amount, as Rev. Cotton had previously assigned over to her all his personal property. An order was then made that the Dennison children be detained at the Naas workhouse pending the determination of the case.

The case was resumed the following Tuesday, March 6th, before Col. Forbes and Mr Bury. A letter was produced from Rev. Cotton asking for a further adjournment of his case, as Dr. Falconer was unavailable. Noting that another adjournment would make it impossible to hear the case at the next assizes, D.I. Supple stated he would not oppose the request, and an adjournment was then granted.

On Wednesday, March 21st, Rev. Cotton came into the boardroom of the Naas workhouse just as the weekly meeting was concluding and asked that the Dennison children be registered as Protestants. When pressed as to the reason why, he admitted that he had found her begging, and she had asked him to take the children, which he agreed to do on the condition that they should be brought up as bible-reading Protestants. This she agreed and delivered the children four or five days later. She herself attended Rev. Cotton's church for four or five Sundays afterwards.

One of the board members, Mr Heffernan, asked if Rev. Cotton promised to bring them up in a respectable manner, to which he replied yes.

Heffernan then asked how it was that there was a public prosecution pending yet again against Cotton for mistreating the children. The board noted that Mary Dennison had baptised one of them in the workhouse as Roman Catholic, and both she herself and her children had been Roman Catholics during their previous stays in the workhouse. Mr Heffernan stated that the religion of children in the workhouse was never tampered with, and the board declined Mr Cotton's request.[12]

Cotton, of course, is not telling the truth. Mrs Dennison asked for nothing from him. It was he who offered to take the children into the now defunct Orphanage, having first admired the boy. And now he has the sheer effrontery to ask that they be brought up as Protestants.

---

[12] Leinster Leader, Sat. 24th Mar 1894

On Tuesday, March 27th, the adjourned case was heard again at the Robertstown Petty Sessions before Col. Forbes and Dr. Neale. D.I. Supple prosecuted on behalf of the Crown, and Dr. Falconer defended.[13]

D.I. Supple stated that on the February 20th, he had entered the Caragh Orphanage with a warrant signed by Col. Forbes, in the company of Head Constable McKeon, Sergeant Nolan, Acting Sergeant Synnott, Constables Donnelly and Mullally, and Dr. McDonagh. In the kitchen, he found Mary Dennison, who was filthy and appeared not to have been washed for a considerable time. When examined by Dr. McDonagh, he noticed she was very thin, her shoulder blades and cheekbones protruding and hair growing between the neck and shoulder blades. She was given bread and butter, which she ate ravenously.

Thomas Dennison was in fair condition, except for his feet, which were tied up with rags and bits of cloth. When Dr. McDonagh removed these, they found the feet to be considerably swollen and 'angry looking'. Both feet had a circular mark in a state of eruption

---

[13] Kildare Observer, Sat. 31st Mar 1894

between the instep and the root of the toes, which were inflamed and encrusted with what appeared to be ointment and dirt. He had a large crack in the right heel and seemed to be suffering from pain. He ate some bread given to him 'like an animal'.

Later, in a shed in the yard, he saw a wooden structure, about 4 feet by 3 feet, with boards across it. Nearby he saw some straw and a dirty blanket. There was also an old, thin rug and a dirty pillow without a cover.

Sheds at the back of the Glebe House used to house the Dennison children.

Head Constable McKeon gave evidence that he entered the orphanage just after D.I. Supple and Dr. McDonagh. The entrance to the kitchen was locked at first, but he observed Mrs Cotton unlocking the door and one of the servants attempting to put a 'bib' on Mary Dennison. He then examined her hair carefully and noticed it was very dirty and crawling with vermin. He stated Thomas Dennison's body seemed cleaner than his sister's, but his feet and head were very dirty.

Sergeant Nolan swore that he entered the hall immediately after D.I. Supple and Dr. McDonagh. Mrs Cotton asked them into the drawing room to wait, but they declined and asked to see the children immediately. She then opened the door leading to the kitchen, where Sgt. Nolan assisted Dr. McDonagh in removing Mary Dennison's clothing. He noticed her body was very dirty, and she had a regular mane of hair about half-an-inch long growing down her backbone. Her head was full of black lice and nits. There was a sore on her right forearm. Her body and arms were very thin. She had broken old boots on her, and her feet were wet. He then assisted Dr. McDonagh in removing the rags from Thomas Dennison's feet, on which he noticed a number of 'angry' sores. The feet and toes were swollen, and there was a large, deep sore on the boy's right heel. He examined his head and found it filled with lice and nits. He then removed the children to the Naas Union workhouse. He denied registering the children there as any religion, as this matter was not his concern.

Dr. McDonagh next gave evidence. He was the Medical Officer of Health to the Robertstown and Kilmeague Dispensary District. He stated that there was some delay in gaining entrance to the kitchen where the children were, as the door was locked, but when he entered, he immediately examined them. He found Mary's face, hair, and ears very dirty and her hair containing vermin. He stripped her to her waist and noticed her collarbone and shoulder blade very prominent and thin, almost to the point of emaciation. She had a very anaemic appearance, from which he concluded she had been much neglected, half-starved, or had received the food of very bad quality. She ate bread and butter ravenously, and it appeared she had not been fed for a considerable time. He noticed a peculiar growth of hair on her back, which might have been due to insufficient nourishment.

He then examined her brother. Both his feet were much inflamed. There were two ulcers on the left foot. The toes were inflamed up to the instep, the feet were of a reddish colour but hard to describe due to the accumulation of dirt and ointment. He thought the inflammation was caused by cold, insufficient covering, general neglect, and the feet had not been properly cared for. The right heel was ulcerated, and he thought it was not right to have the child walking about, he should have been in bed. When asked if the sores on the feet were chilblains, Dr. McDonagh replied that he could not make a positive diagnosis due to their filthy condition.

Mrs Ellen Geoghegan of Ballymore Eustace, aunt to the children, swore that she knew that they went to Mr Cotton's orphanage about the 3rd of May 1893. They were then in good condition. Mary was fairly fat, and Thomas was a very fat, plump child. She stated her sister was weak-minded, and she herself had reared Mary for three years until she parted with her when the child was taken to the orphanage. Both children were born in the workhouse. Her sister was there for two years until last May. She had been a general servant but could not say how long she had been out of work.

About six years previously, her sister had a house in Ballymore Eustace but had been from her situation to the workhouse for the past three years. She was now in Ballymore.

The case was then adjourned until Tuesday, 3rd April, to a special Petty Session court held in Robertstown. The magistrates present were Col. Forbes in the chair and Dr. Neale. D.I. Supple prosecuted, and Dr. Falconer defended. Mr P. J. McCann appeared for the ISPCC.

Dr. Smyth, Medical Officer of the Naas Union, corroborated the evidence given earlier as the condition of the children when admitted to the workhouse. He described their condition with the help of four photographs which were taken shortly after the children's admission to the workhouse. He continued to see the children until the present time and observed that they had considerably improved while in the workhouse.

Dr. Falconer then applied to the case against Mrs Cotton, which was dismissed on the grounds that she had been previously acquitted due to a lack of evidence against her. D.I. Supple objected as she was the owner of the orphanage, and he could prove this. He said she was assigned over the property in order to evade any fines that might be imposed. He had seized goods to settle a fine imposed in the previous conviction and auctioned the same. Mrs Cotton had bought back the seized goods for the sum of £88.

At the conclusion of the evidence, the bench formally returned Mr Cotton for trial at the ensuing assizes, in his own bail of £100 and two sureties of £50 each.

County Kildare Assizes, Naas, Thur. 19th July 1894

The case against Cotton was heard before Lord Chief Justice Sir Peter O'Brien, Baronet. Mr C. Molloy Q. C. and Mr O. B. Hamilton (instructed by Mr Grove White) were prosecuted, and Dr. Falconer (instructed by Mr J. J. O'Mahony) defended.

Much of the evidence presented was the same as that reported previously at the petty session's court in Robertstown.

The witnesses for the prosecution were: Mary Dennison (née Corcoran, the children's mother), D.I. Supple, Sergeant Nolan, and Head-Constable McKeon (Robertstown police barracks), Dr. McDonagh (Dispensary Doctor, Kilmeague, Dr. Sale's replacement) and Dr. Smyth (Naas Union workhouse).

Witnesses for the defence were: Jane McGrath (Mr Cotton's servant) and her daughter Lizzie, Louisa Wright (one month in Mr Cotton's service, July & August 1893), Mr Robert Carter (apothecary in Naas), and his assistant Joseph Soden, Miss Annan (Matron of the South Dublin Union) and lastly Mrs Cotton and Rev. Cotton themselves.

Mary Dennison stated both her children were born in the workhouse at Naas. She met Cotton at Sallins station in April 1893, two days after she had left the workhouse, and he said to her, "what a fine boy Tommy was", then telling her she would be imprisoned for begging, and he would relieve her of the children. The following day she made her way to Caragh orphanage, where she met Mrs Cotton, who took her in. She remained at the orphanage for a month until Rev. Cotton found her a position with Captain Bunberry in Carlow (Lisnavagh, Rathvilly).

When she left her children, she claimed they were clean and strong. When they were rescued, she said that they were in such a state she "did not know them". When asked about her religion, she said she was Catholic until he "turned me". She said she was now a Catholic again but that her head "often gets bad" and she frequently lost her memory. She climbed the walls of the workhouse owing to her treatment there and used to "go about the country, leaving the children behind". When she first met Rev. Cotton, she did not know him until he approached her. She did not beg from him, as she "only begged from people she knew".

Michael Anderson, a porter at Naas workhouse, confirmed that Mary Dennison entered the workhouse on 29th September 1892 and was discharged on 14th April 1893. The children were readmitted into the workhouse on 20th February 1894. Mary Byrne, a workhouse official, stated that the children left the house "clean and fat", but when they were returned, they were very poor, and their hair was in a filthy condition.

D.I. Supple repeated the evidence he had given earlier at the Robertstown Petty Sessions Court, describing the condition in which he found the children. He stated it was not his first visit to the orphanage as he had previously visited in May 1893 with a warrant to seize goods resulting from the non-payment of the £400 fine imposed in the earlier conviction at Belfast. The goods seized were auctioned at Robertstown on 30th May 1893 and were bought back by Mrs Cotton for the sum of £88.

Sergeant Nolan confirmed the evidence he had given previously as the state of the children and said that when brought to the workhouse, the little girl weighed 34lbs, 14ozs, and the boy 27lbs 7ozs. He also heard the little girl say that the 'bed' they slept in was found in the stable.

Head Constable McKeon stated that when he tried to gain access to the kitchen, where the children were being hurriedly cleaned and dressed, he found the door locked and saw a key in it, which Mrs Cotton denied in her evidence, stating that the kitchen door was never locked as the key was missing for the past 25 years.

Dr. McDonagh also repeated the evidence he gave at Robertstown as the state of the children and his examination of them. Dr. Smyth also repeated his testimony about the condition of the children when admitted into the workhouse.

During Rev. Cotton's cross-examination, Mr Molloy asked him if he had a boy named Ross in the orphanage in 1883. Dr. Falconer immediately objected, but Mr Molloy then produced a log with a chain attached, which caused a sensation in court.

Lord Chief Justice Sir Peter O'Brien reviewed the evidence, and the jury then retired to consider their verdict. After a short absence, they returned a verdict of guilty on all counts against Rev. Cotton but acquitted Mrs Cotton. Dr. Falconer asked that a fine be imposed instead of imprisonment, which would be injurious to Rev. Cotton's health.

Irish Examiner 1841-current, 20.07.1894, page 5

THE CAROGH ORPHANAGE

ANOTHER SENTENCE ON REV. MR. COTTON.

———

Naas, Thursday.

At the Kildare Assizes to-day Rev. Samuel Cotton of the Carogh Orphanage, was sentenced to twelve months' imprisonment for ill-treating two children. Mrs. Cotton, against whom a similar charge was preferred, was acquitted. The Chief Justice, in sentencing the prisoner, said neither peer nor peasant nor anybody else in Kildare had any connection with the orphanage.

He added: I never found myself so profoundly moved.

I rejoice to find that your wife has been acquitted. It is the verdict that I should have awarded myself. But whilst the jury has acquitted her, they have found you guilty, and in the verdict with which I entirely agree. I told the jury not to let any sectarian feeling influence them in considering the case, and I believe that in consideration of the case, they were entirely free from all sectarian prejudice. They have acquitted your wife.

They have convicted you, and as I have already stated in that conviction, I entirely agree.

Sir, you were found guilty before. Already you have been found guilty in the city of Belfast of a similar offence. You received on that occasion the punishment of six months imprisonment, and you were subjected to a fine, pursuant to the sentence of the Lord Chief Baron, a most humane judge. Neither the sentence which was passed upon you on that occasion nor your sacred calling, which I respect, induced you to relinquish what I must designate as your evil ways and notwithstanding the certificate of the eminent medical men, Sir George Porter, and Mr Fitzgerald.

You appear to me now in fairly good health. Having regard now to the fact that you were sentenced before for a similar offence to six months imprisonment and that punishment has not had the deterrent effect, which is the object of punishment, it is my painful, most painful duty to sentence you to twelve months imprisonment. I do so with great regret. I sentence you to twelve months imprisonment on each count, but I make the sentence concurrent so that you are not sentenced to more than twelve months imprisonment in all. Should it transpire that the sentence is too severe and that your state of health and your eyesight are imperilled, it will be open to you to appeal to the Executive.

As to the action of the Executive, I cannot in any way predicate. I am responsible for my own action only and for my own duty, and in the discharge of that duty, I sentence you to twelve months imprisonment. Remove the reverend gentleman.

Rev. Mr Cotton: My lord. I wish to say ....

The Chief Justice: I cannot hear you, sir! Remove the reverend gentleman.

Dr. Falconer: I am desired to ask your lordship that you should make it a condition of your order that the Rev. Mr Cotton should be treated as a first-class misdemeanant.

The Chief Justice: No, I did not say hard labour. I said a year's imprisonment.

Mrs Cotton was deeply affected by the result. The Rev. Mr Cotton left the court in custody, apparently not very much concerned.

The business closed at 20 minutes to nine o'clock.

The Rev. Mr Cotton was removed to the train station in an open carriage with other prisoners. There was much jeering and shouting outside the courthouse. Hence to Dublin with other prisoners by the train, which arrived at half past ten o'clock, and he was then taken to Kilmainham. He will be taken to Kilkenny Jail today.

It might be noted here that prison conditions in the late nineteenth century were extremely harsh indeed. Prisoners were, in effect, kept locked down in solitary confinement for 23 hours every 24, given only an hour's recreation per day.

Now known as Prisoner 468. He is measured 5ft 3in height and weighing 123lbs. Grey hair, grey eyes, and complexion fresh, Cotton is sent to start his sentence.

The following day the papers were full of reports of Cotton's imprisonment, and, needless to say, by now, he had lost the ranking of Reverend. Many of the headlines carrying captions such as "Common criminal". Other headlines suggesting that he be sent to Australia like many Irish people had been sent in previous years for lesser offences.

There is also now mounting pressure for the Representative Church Body (RCB) to act on Cotton's repetitive criminal behaviour.

While in Kilkenny prison, Cotton kept notes by way of pasted cuttings. Here we see some letters from seriously misguided people offering sympathy and giving him money.

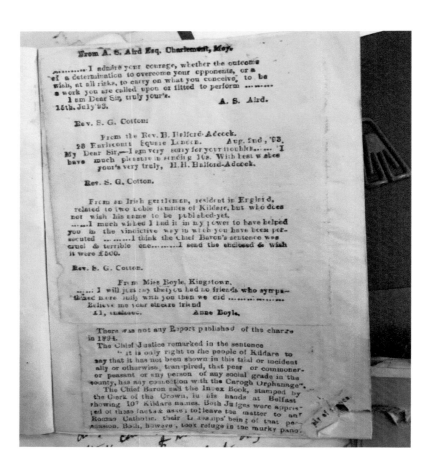

From A. S. Aird Esq. Charlemont, Moy.

.... I admire your courage, whether the outcome
of a determination to overcome your opponents, or a
wish, at all risks, to carry on what you conceive, to be
a work you are called upon or fitted to perform ....
I am Dear Sir, truly your's.
15th. July '93.   A. S. Aird.

Rev. S. G. Cotton:

From the Rev. B. Halford-Adcock.
28 Earlscourt Square London.   Aug. 2nd, '93.
My Dear Sir,—I am very sorry for your trouble......... I
have much pleasure in sending 10s. With best wishes
your's very truly,   H. H. Halford-Adcock.

Rev. S. G. Cotton.

From an Irish gentleman, resident in England,
related to two noble families of Kildare, but who does
not wish his name to be published-yet.
......I much wished I had it in my power to have helped
you in the vindictive way in which you have been persecuted ....I think the Chief Baron's sentence was
cruel & terrible one..........I send the enclosed & wish
it were £500.

Rev. S. G. Cotton.

From Miss Boyle, Kingstown.
...... I will just say that you had no friends who sympathised more fully with you than we did ....
Believe me your sincere friend
£1, enclosed.   Anne Boyle.

There was not any Report published of the charge
in 1894.
The Chief Justice remarked in the sentence
" it is only right to the people of Kildare to
say that it has not been shown in this trial or incident
ally or otherwise, transpired, that peer or commoner-
or peasant or any person of any social grade in the
county, has any connection with the Carogh Orphanage".
The Chief Baron call the Index Book, stamped by
the Clerk of the Crown, in his hands at Belfast
showing 107 Kildare names. Both Judges were appris-
ed of these facts & assu to leave the matter to any
Roman Catholic, their Lordships' being of that permission. Both, however, took refuge in the murky pano.

"From A. S. Aird Esq. Charlemont, Moy. "I admire your courage, whether the outcome of a determination to overcome your opponents, or a wish, at all risks, to carry on what you conceive, to be a work you are called upon or fitted to perform... I am Dear Sir, truly your's. 15 July 1893. A. S. Aird."

"From the Rev H Halford-Adcock. 28 Earls Court Square London. Aug 2 1893. "My Dear Sir, I am very sorry for your trouble. I have much pleasure in sending 10s. With best wishes your's very truly, H. H. Halford-Adcock."

"From an Irish gentleman, resident in England, related to two noble families of Kildare, but who does not wish his name to be published yet... I much wished I had it in my power to have helped you in the vindictive way in which you have been persecuted ... I think the Chief Baron's sentence was cruel & terrible one ... I send the enclosed & wish it were £500."

"From Miss Boyle, Kingstown, ... "I will just say that you had no friends who sympathised more fully with you than we did ...believe me your sincere friend. £1 enclosed. Anne Boyle."

Another paper was asking through the columns how it is that the rector of Caragh, who has recently been convicted of cruelty to children and sentenced to twelve months imprisonment, appears to be able to defy ecclesiastical law?

"He has already had a similar experience, but in spite of it, he walks out of prison back to the charge of his parish. Is this process to be repeated at the end of another twelve months, it asked? What is his Grace Lord Plunket doing? What also are the Protestant Defence Association doing in the matter? Are there no aggrieved parishioners in Caragh? Does the Irish Church require a special organisation to defend it from Canon Smith while Mr Cotton is allowed to pep back and forward with impunity between the prison and the pulpit? It is very strange and unaccountable and requires expiation.[14]

Yours

M.A., T.C.D"

---

[14] The Freemans Journal

10 – Church Authority finally react. Loss of Glebe and all privileges. Retirement to Bray and Death

The Representative Church Body are eventually roused to action. This can't be overlooked any longer. It would seem that after some consultation and not a little buck passing and procrastination, a decision was made to terminate Cotton's contract with them. They gave him an ultimatum.

The legal committee of the Representative Body has just issued the following report on the case of Rev. S. G. Cotton, Rector of Caragh, who was twice convicted of gross cruelty to children committed to his care.

The legal committee has considered the following resolution of the Representative Body, which was passed on the 17th of October 1894.

"That the application of the Rev. S. G. Cotton for release from duty be referred to the legal committee to report on the whole question of the Representative Body."

In dealing with this case, the legal committee are of the opinion that Mr Cotton is subject to the (Irish Church Act, s.20) to the ecclesiastical law of Ireland, and to the rules, discipline, and ordinances of the Church of Ireland, as they existed in 1869 with and subject to the modifications and alterations thereof made by the General Synod, including the jurisdiction of the tribunals of the Church, and the provisions of the Church Statute of the 14th of April, 1893.

Upon this hypothesis, three questions arise:

1. Whether Mr Cotton has offended against these?

2. If so, what penalty has he incurred?

3. Can such penalties be enforced in the Courts of the Church or the temporal tribunals?

The legal committee are of the opinion:

- That the cruelty of which the temporal Courts have convicted Mr Cotton on two occasions, taken in connection with the fact of the convictions themselves and the scandal arising there from (independently of his non-residence and neglect of duty), constitutes an offence against the present ecclesiastical law of the Church of Ireland.

- That he is liable to be deprived of his office and benefits for these offences.

- That a sentence of this effect can be obtained in the Court of the General Synod, which, if necessary, can be made operative in the ordinary tribunals of the country and the glebe recovered by means of ejectment.

Samuel Cotton has lost his title of Reverent and Vicar. By now, he is identified as Prisoner 468. As he attempts to contrive his way out of prison, the medical officers and prison officials of Kilkenny Prison are having none of it, however, determined he may be to save the Glebe House from the hands of the Representative Church Body.

In these unedited prison records, Mr Cotton tells of "rushes of blood to his head." It seems that two of his sisters had recently died suffering from depression, and these "rushes of blood to the head" led to their death. Cotton is fearful that he might have the same faith if imprisoned for too long. This, of course, is just fabricated nonsense.

He informs the RCB that he is due a large sum of money left to his wife from Mr John Irvine's fourteen-year previous 1881. We have seen the Court Case contesting this version of his will so as the Cottons appear to be the sole beneficiaries of Irvine's will. The jury dismissed this as a forgery created by the Cottons. In turn, the Cottons had to pay costs for the Court Case.

Cotton is now desperate and is at the mercy of the goodwill of the RCB. Still defiant, he writes back to them with the following counter-proposal.

Mr Cotton has proposed to resign his benefits upon the terms:

- Continuing to receive the interest payable to him under an agreement dated the 11th of October 1878.
- Retaining possession of the Glebe House and land during his lifetime.

- Being paid after the death of his wife a profit rent of £52.10s bequeathed by the late Mr Irvine for the benefit of Caragh Parish, subject to a life interest vested in Mrs Cotton.

It appears, however, from a letter addressed by Mr Cotton on the 5th of November 1894 to the secretary of the Dublin Diocesan Council, that he now waives the last mentioned claim presumably because it's based on a forgery.

The legal committee are of an opinion that in point of law, all these claims would be forfeited in the event of a sentence of deprivation being passed, but they venture to suggest that, having regard to the circumstances within the endowment fund was created, the interest of which is payable to Mr Cotton under the said agreement. Mr Cotton should be informed that, if he shall forthwith resign his benefits, and surrender the possession of his Glebe House to the Representative Body, the Representative Body will continue to pay him the said interest during his life. The legal committee thinks that Mr Cotton ought at the same time to be informed that if he declines to accept this offer, proceedings will at once be taken in the

Church Courts to deprive him of his office and benefits.[15]

This, if ever, was a Hopkins Choice. Either get out now and be paid his interest. Or stay on in the Glebe House, be ejected, and get nothing.

Samuel Cotton was released from Kilkenny Goal in July 1895 and stripped of his secret office. A man who was made famous for his revolting crimes, his litigious nature, his propensity to broadcast his every move in the broadsheets of the day, and his psychopathic, narcissistic nature, has finally been disgraced. Now for a change, he goes silently into the mist, living the rest of his days in a two-bedroom cottage at Green Park Bray, County Wicklow beside his birthplace.

---

[15] Belfast News Letter

House belonging to Cotton in Bray, where he lived out his final two years and where he died.

Cotton's only death notice in the papers appeared in the Kildare Observer. It is stark and, I think, even for its day, quite unusual.

> *"Kildare Observer and Eastern Counties Advertiser. Saturday 8 September 1900. COTTON – August 31ˢᵗ, at his residence, Green Park, Bray, Rev S G Cotton, after a long and painful illness, aged 77."*

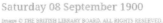

OOTTON—August 31st, at his residence, Green Park, Bray, Rev S G Cotton, after a long and painful illness, aged 77.

Whose idea was it to insert "after a long and painful illness"? Was that Eliza's contribution? Or was the Editor just being vindictive?

Samuel George Cotton died on 31st August 1900. Unusually, there were no obituaries or funeral arrangements entered in the newspapers. No "deeply regretted, in the loving arms" and so on. He was seventy-seven years old. To the best of our knowledge, he is buried behind Caragh Church, and a tombstone was erected there, naming himself and Eliza up to recent times. It would appear that this was unlawfully demolished sometime in the 1980s to make way for development.

Here is his death certificate:

31st August 1900 Green Park Bray	Samuel George Cotton	m	married	77 years	Protestant Clergyman	Atrophy of Heart 1 year Albuminuria 3 months Certified	Thomas Nolan Present at Death Green Park	September Tenth TB/900	Cecil Brew Registrar		

As is so often the case with death certificates, this one is not correct. He did not have "atrophy of heart" for one year. We know from his prison records that Cotton had atrial fibrillation for at least 10 years before he died. This would have made him very short of breath and account for his 'long and painful illness'.

By his time of death, Cotton was a wealthy landlord of considerable means. Here we see him offering to rent two houses. This was in addition to the one he already had in Bray, where he died.

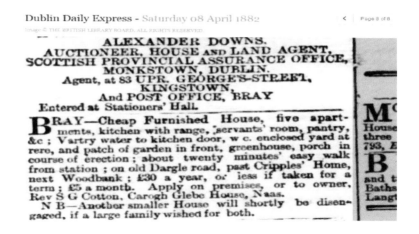

"Dublin Daily Express – Saturday 8 April 1882. BRAY – Cheap Furnished House, five apartments, kitchen with range, 'servants' room, pantry, ... Vartry water to kitchen door, w.c. enclosed yard at rear, and patch of garden in front,

greenhouse, porch in course of erection; about twenty minutes' easy walk from station; on old Dargle Road, past Cripples' Home, next Woodbank; £30 a year, or less if taken for a term; £5 a month. Apply on premises, or to owner, Rev S G Cotton, Carogh Glebe House, Naas.

N B – Another smaller House will shortly be disengaged, if a large family wished for both."

Eliza outlived her husband Samuel, by some 14 years. Aged 91, she died a wealthy woman at her home at 42 Belmont Avenue, Donnybrook, Dublin 4 on Sept 19th, 1914. She left an estate of some £2,642 to her friend Letitia F Myles. The will was probated on the 19th of March 1915.

****

Some of the Children that went through Caragh Orphanage.

Let us remember them.

Children rescued in 1891.

BROWN, Thomas

Hidden in an attic in Dublin.

BURNETT, Alexander (12)

Born 19 Feb 1879

BURNETT, Annie (17)

Born 17 Jun 1874.

Too old to be sent to the orphanage so was employed as a servant at the Glebe House.

BURNETT, Elizabeth (3)

Born 15 Feb 1888

BURNETT, James (10)

Born 6 Jun 1881

BURNETT, Mary (10 months)

Born 11 Dec 1890

BURNETT, Minnie (5)

Born 25 May 1886

BURNETT, Samuel (8)

Born 27 Apr 1883

CARSON, Ellen (2)

CLEARY, Ann

CLEARY, John (8)

COLLINS (McCollum), Thomas (3 months)

Died two days after being rescued from Caragh at the Orthopaedic Hospital, Great Brunswick Street, Dublin, on 11 Nov 1891.

CULLEN, Thomas

DENNISON, Mary (7)

DENNISON, Thomas (3)

HAYNE, Thomas

HEADLEY, Charles

HURLEY (Harley), Mary (3 months)

KELLY, Ellen (13)

KING, Annie (13)

Was made to work as a "nurse" in the orphanage.

LYNCH, Kathleen (9 months)

Died at the Orphanage.

MILLS, Mary (13)

Nursed the younger children.

NOLAN, Thomas (15)

Said he was 13 years in the orphanage in 1891.

NOLAN, William (Willie) (9)

NORTON, Henry (4)

PARKER, Adelaide (13)

Was made to work as a "nurse" in the orphanage.

QUILLETT, Charles (4)

ROSS, John (8)

SAVAGE, Bernard

Hidden in an attic in Dublin.

STEELE, Robert

TUTTY, Elizabeth

Said she was "a servant at the Glebe House for 2.5 years."

WALKER, Patience (4)

WALLACE, Benjamin (6)

WARREN, Thomas (5)

WHITNEY, Thomas (5)

WILLETT (Wills or Willis), Mary (13)

Hidden in an attic in Dublin.

WINTER, Eliza (4)

Children who previously lived at the orphanage:

BOYD, George

At the orphanage in 1879.

BROWN, William

Died 7 Dec 1879, aged 8 (aged 6 according to the death certificate) – was at the orphanage since he was a baby, having come there from the Rotunda Hospital, according to Mrs Margaret Douglas (née Condell), ie. Since 1871, or 1873.

Rev. Cotton used to beat William Brown once a day before he put him in an ice bath days before Christmas of 1879 and left him on bare floorboards under broken windows to die.

CLARKE, Joseph

At the orphanage in 1879, aged 7. He was 19 in 1891 and a printer by trade when giving evidence against Cotton, in the Brown manslaughter case.

CUFFE, Joseph

Aged 23 in 1891, a tram conductor who gave evidence at the Curragh Petty Session on 14 Nov 1891.

DYER (Murphy), Joseph

At the orphanage in 1879. Gave evidence at the Curragh PS. Living in Edinburgh at the time of the Court Case.

GIBBONS, Peter

At the orphanage in 1879. Gave evidence at the Curragh PS.

NOLAN, Thomas

At the orphanage in 1879. Still there in 1891 – was 13 years there.

SKERRITT, George

At the orphanage in 1879.

THOMPSON, Henry

Slept on the floor with Brown.

WILMOT (Walsh), James

At the orphanage in 1879. Aged 22 in 1891.

We don't have names for all of the children who died at Caragh. Some were buried in the churchyard of Caragh Church and were exhumed and reinterred in 1976 in Millicent Churchyard.

THE END

~~~~~~~~~~~~~~~~~~~~~~~~~~~~~~~

References

1. Dublin Evening Mail, 16 May 1866 20

2. Kildare Observer and Eastern Counties Advertiser Caragh Glebe House, March 19th 1883 46

3. The Irish Times- Saturday 15th September 1883 71

4. Annie, born 17 Jun 1874 / Alexander, born 19 Feb 1879 / James, born 6 Jun 1881 / Samuel, born 27 Apr 1883 / Mary (Minnie) born 25 May 1886 / Elizabeth, born 15 Feb 1888 / Mary, born 11 Dec 1890. Except for the eldest child, the name of the father is registered as Robert Burnett, labourer, and the mother as Mary Burnett, formerly Moffat. Subsequently, on 19 Aug 1891, Bridget McCusker, who had been present for four of the births, made a statutory declaration stating that the parents were not legally married, and this was noted retrospectively. 85

5. Freeman's Journal, Mon. 9 Nov 1891 100

6. On hearing of the news surrounding Caragh orphanage two former inmates, James Walsh and William Goff, came forward to state that,